SABINE'S ODYSSEY

A HIDDEN CHILD AND HER DUTCH RESCUERS

AGNES SCHIPPER

a|p

ISBN: 9789493231962 (ebook)

ISBN: 9789493231948 (paperback)

ISBN: 9789493231955 (hardcover)

Publisher: Amsterdam Publishers, The Netherlands

info@amsterdampublishers.com

Sabine's Odyssey is part of the series

Jewish Children in the Holocaust

Cover image: Andreas and Sabine, Breslau (1934)

CONTENTS

To my parents, Sabine and Cor

and to the memory of Andreas Fröhlich

INTRODUCTION

Odyssey: a long wandering or voyage, usually marked by many changes in fortune. - **Merriam-Webster Dictionary**

My mother Sabine was a hidden child during WWII. The reason she had to go underground was hidden from me until I was 20. The family secrecy was understandable for a generation that had lived through the atrocities of the Nazi era and wanted to shield future generations from similar horrors.

Sabine, the only daughter of a seemingly "assimilated" German family, was raised as a Catholic. Her odyssey began in 1939 at age 12 when she traveled on the Kindertransport to England. In the space of one year, Sabine would attend four schools, each taught in a different language. Her parents had her and her brother Andreas leave England to join them in the Netherlands while they awaited visas to join relatives in the United States. The visas did not materialize and the family became trapped after the Germans invaded.

Sabine survived the war by being hidden in nine different places in the Netherlands from 1942 to 1945. Her parents who hid separately from her for most of the war also survived. Her brother, her only sibling, did not.

Later in her life, Sabine's odyssey became a determined search for any wartime records about her brother. She sought reassurance that Andreas "did not just vanish off this earth," as she put it. She was 14 when she last saw him being led away by two Dutch policemen working for the Gestapo in Amsterdam. She was 71 when she made the journey to Mauthausen, the gruesome concentration camp in Austria where he perished. I would continue that second odyssey of searching for records about Andreas after her death in 2017.

The story has harrowing parts; it's not easy to read about the cruelties people inflict on their fellow humans. These parts will be hard to leaf through, but I hope also hard to forget. The hideousness of antisemitism should never be forgotten. But the story also has uplifting parts about the kindness and courage of people who risked their lives to save others. It is also a love story between a refugee and one of her rescuers, my father. Only in the cataclysm of a world war would two people from such different backgrounds have intersected: a German lawyer's daughter and a Dutch bulb grower. This book is a tribute to my mother's indomitable spirit and resilience and to my father's bravery and steadfastness.

Sabine's story has relevance today given resurgent antisemitism, the rise of autocrats who stir fear and hatred, and the scapegoating of refugees and immigrants. My hope as the daughter of a hidden child is that Sabine's story not only will inspire readers to speak out against antisemitism and other forms of discrimination when they encounter such, but also that they will feel more compassion toward refugees.

Finally, for anyone who might doubt Sabine's story, I have ample proof of its veracity. My mother was a pack-rat, an extreme saver who kept letters, photos, notarized declarations and many other documents that confirm every detail of her story. This irrefutable proof will be donated to and archived at the United States Holocaust Memorial Museum in Washington, D.C.

1

TANTE ELLA. THE "FAMILY SECRET" REVEALED

By the time I first met Tante (German for "aunt") Ella, she was in her eighties. Her back was bent with age, shortening her already petite frame. But her mind was sharp; she was friendly, lively and charming. We met in May 1969, near the end of my junior year of college abroad in England at the London School of Economics. I was 20.

Ella was the widow of my great-uncle, Eugen Fröhlich. Tante Ella lived in West Hampstead, an upscale section of London, in a beautiful apartment filled with antiques and Persian rugs. She dressed elegantly in a knit suit with a silk scarf. Her eyes were a deep, sparkling sapphire blue and her smile, warm and slightly mischievous. Her white-gray hair was carefully coifed. She treated me to a delicious meal of filet mignon at an expensive restaurant nearby. Fine dining was a rare and welcome treat for me, a student who subsisted on cafeteria meals and cheap restaurant fare.

What I remember most, though, about Tante Ella is our conversation at her home after the fancy meal. I sat in her living room across from her, she in a comfortable, upholstered chair.

"You know about Andreas, don't you?"

"Yes, I do. My mother's brother. He died in a concentration camp," I replied.

"They took him because he was Jewish."

I sat up straighter in my chair and turned my head to the side, trying to hide my surprise. But my eyes must have widened and betrayed me when I looked back into Ella's blue eyes.

"You didn't know?"

"No."

My mother had told me that her family had had to leave Germany and that her brother had been taken away because her father had spoken out against the Nazis. I had no reason to question that explanation. I had been raised Catholic and had no inkling about a Jewish background.

Tante Ella had inadvertently revealed a family secret, unaware that it was a secret. Family secrets are easier to keep when you grow up an ocean apart from your European relatives. Looking back now, I think, *Poor Tante Ella*. She must have been so uncomfortable to have been placed in this awkward position. She quickly changed the topic of conversation to something utterly forgettable. I left her lovely apartment shortly afterwards.

It was a warm spring evening, just after sunset. Many Londoners were still lingering outside, sitting on benches or strolling through the nearby park. I headed down the stairs to the tube (underground railway) station to take a subway ride back to my apartment in Hampstead Heath. As the train departed and rumbled through the tunnel, I thought about the revelation. After the initial shock, I could not help smiling to myself as the train slowed, approaching the next station. I was pleased and a little proud to learn that my family history now stretched two to three thousand years further back. From A.D. well into B.C. *I have Jewish heritage*, I thought to myself. *How cool.* But I had so many questions, starting with, *Why was this fact kept a secret from me in the first place?*

Tante Ella certainly could not tell me why because she had not been aware it was a secret. I quickly became preoccupied with final exams, packing up and saying goodbye to my LSE friends. When the school term ended a few weeks later, I left England for a summer of travel. I flew first to Israel, then went by boat to Greece and from there traveled by rail and bus northward through much of continental Europe.

Near the end of my summer of travels, I made my way to West Germany to visit my maternal grandparents, "Oma" (grandma) Edith and "Opa" (grandpa) Georg Fröhlich. (In those Cold War years, Europe was divided into communist-run "Eastern Europe" and democratic "Western Europe.") My mother's parents had rented the lower floor of a comfortable, newer home in the small town of Bühlertal in Schwarzwald (the Black Forest) for the summer. Their apartment was in the last house on the road, situated at the crest of a steep hill in the foothills of the Black Forest. "The end of the world," my grandmother used to call the view from their apartment. So beautiful and peaceful. The scene from their living room was so picturesque: a green valley dotted with homes and farms below, the adjacent hills blanketed with dense layers of dark pine trees. I loved the way the clouds wrapped over and into the woods like a gossamer shawl. We were that high in the mountainous forest.

The living room couch faced the picture window, whose sill was dotted with a collection of thriving house plants in ceramic pots, carefully maintained by Klara, my grandparents' housekeeper. My grandmother's Biedermeier writing desk was in the front left-hand corner, with the black-and-white television on its stand nearby. In the back right corner was my grandfather's high-back, faded-red upholstered chair. The chair was positioned next to a large Telefunken radio that he could reach easily to tune into his favorite news and music programs. No one in the household dared speak when the radio news was on; that time was sacrosanct for him. Next to the radio was a reel-to-reel tape deck that my grandfather, blind from macular degeneration and glaucoma by 1969, used to listen to tape-recorded readings of books that arrived by mail.

My Oma was a very social and elegant woman, always stylishly dressed and often on the phone talking with friends. She was a would-be matchmaker, convincing a friend to bring her son to the Black Forest to meet me and promoting him to me as ever so handsome, intelligent and *witzig* (witty). I had no interest in a German beau and was unjustifiably rude to the poor fellow, leaving the room abruptly. My grandmother was justifiably disappointed. At 20, I lacked the grace to indulge her match-making wishes for just a little bit. I also remember my grandmother as a very anxious person. We learned never to tell her when a family member planned to take a flight because she would fret endlessly about the plane crashing.

I had spent the summer of my 11th year in the Black Forest with my Oma and Opa. I thought my Opa Fröhlich was the smartest man I had ever met, with a Renaissance-like breadth of interests. I could give him any three random words, in English, German or Dutch, and he would weave them into a poem. I remember giggling as an 11-year-old would when I listed "toilet paper" as one of the three words, yet he worked it into a verse. When I visited him in 1969 and told him about my summer of travel, he asked me if a particular painting (whose title and artist I now forget) was still at the Pitti Palace in Florence. Yes, I told him, it was; I had seen the painting there. I was amazed at his memory.

He loved opera, including Wagner whom I found impossibly long and ponderous. (He disagreed with me on that.) A theater enthusiast, he could quote Schiller and Shakespeare. Even late in life, he could recite long passages from plays in which he had performed in his youth. He had considered an acting career but his eldest brother persuaded him to consider a legal career instead, advising Georg that "a second-rate lawyer lives but a second-rate actor starves." Georg, however, also loved the law and would become a first-rate lawyer and judge.

In his youth, he was a mountain climber. He was a tall man, with brown eyes and his dark gray hair combed back. In a painting and photographs of him in his judge's robes, he looks stern and

4

formidable. But with his grandchildren he was approachable and delightful. When I spent that summer with my grandparents as a child, I ate breakfast earlier than my Opa. Every morning, I would carefully remove my soft-boiled egg from its shell, turn the shell upside down and place it in his egg cup. And every morning he would feign great surprise to crack open an empty shell.

But back to 1969. Although very tempted to do so, I did not ask my grandparents about the family history. I sensed instinctively that asking about this would have been wrong and upsetting for them. I thought there must be some good reason for the secrecy. My mother should be the one to explain it to me. My questions would therefore have to wait until I returned to the US at the end of the summer to begin my final year of college at New York University (NYU). I never saw Tante Ella again.

Back in the US after a year abroad, I confronted my mother when we finally had time alone together. Private time is not easy in a household with four younger siblings—a sister and three brothers. My mother and I were in the living room of our home on 47 Danner Avenue in Harrison, New York. The room was furnished in 1950s Scandinavian style: chairs with spindle wooden legs; a love-seat with tweed upholstery and side-arms of dark wood; the stereo housed in a large dark cabinet near the door to the pantry; the portable television with rabbit ears in the opposite corner. A rim of dark wood high on the walls all around the room, holding antique porcelain plates and vases.

"Why didn't you tell me Opa Fröhlich and your family were Jewish?"

My mother looked up at me. She took a deep breath but stayed calm. "Who told you?"

That was confirmation, in and of itself, I thought to myself, before answering, "Tante Ella. But what about my question? Why didn't you tell me?"

"My mother made me promise never to tell you children about it."

"But why?"

"Because she did not want the curse of a Jewish background to follow the next generation."

My mother told me that my Oma had destroyed evidence about our Jewish heritage. She had incinerated the last will and testament of Adolph Fröhlich, my great-grandfather. Adolph was the last person on either side of her family (maternal and paternal) to be a practicing Jew. My mother never met him; he had died decades before she was born, when her own father was only 13 years old, leaving him an orphan under the care of older siblings.

Mom's maternal grandparents, Margarete Nissen née Borchert and Dr. Franz Nissen, were not practicing Jews. Margarete had registered her children (including my grandmother) as Protestants. My mother was raised as a Catholic—Baptism, First Holy Communion, Confirmation, schooled by Ursuline nuns, married in a Catholic church. Before the Nazis came to power, her German relatives would have been described as "assimilated Jews." But the assimilation turned out to be an illusion.

My mother told me it was hard, at times, to comply with the promise she had made to her mother, especially when she heard antisemitic remarks. She brought up as an example something I had said two years earlier, when I was a college sophomore. I had told her then about an NYU classmate who had commented that, "Jews aren't happy unless they are being persecuted." She thought I had endorsed this opinion. She, of course, disagreed with it, but said nothing at the time about our own heritage. I cringed, feeling mortified. I explained to my mother that I didn't accept this view; I was just quoting what a classmate had said, someone I had encountered at a meeting of the Cardinal Newman Society (a Catholic education organization) at NYU.

My mother did not speak openly about her family's Jewish history until after Oma Edith died in 1979. Then she began her quest in earnest to learn more about what had happened to her brother, researching the Holocaust. She accumulated her own small library on the subject, with texts in German, Dutch and English.

Decades pass. For me, college graduation, working a year in New York City, graduate school in California, marriage, journalism career, two children, move to Minnesota, two more children, law school and law career, move to North Carolina, then back to Minnesota. Finally, in 1998, I take the time to learn details about my mother's childhood and the family's Jewish history during a trip with Mom to Mauthausen, the concentration camp where my mother's brother perished in 1941 at the age of 20.

2

SEARCHING FOR HER BROTHER'S NAME

In May 1998, my mother and I went on a train trip from Amsterdam to Mauthausen, Austria. The trip was organized by the *Vriendenkring* (Circle of Friends) Mauthausen, a Dutch organization for the friends and families of the victims of the Mauthausen concentration camp.

The journey was the culmination of years of study and effort by Mom to try to discover what had happened to her brother. By the 1990s, she had begun to focus her quest on locating her brother's name on some wartime documentation or list, some official physical record of his arrest, deportation and death—some comfort that he not be an anonymous, unrecorded victim among the millions in the Holocaust.

The Fröhlichs had learned about Andreas' death verbally. Mom had a vivid memory of that moment: "I see her still [Bella Dispek, a family friend living in the same apartment building in Amsterdam], walking up the stairs to come into our room with the news that Andreas was "on the list." The list was of the most recent deaths at Mauthausen camp, posted weekly in the offices of the *Joodse Raad* (the Jewish Council, set up by Nazis) in Amsterdam. The Fröhlichs never received formal written notification of his death.

Mom gave me a thick folder of materials she had gathered in her search for records about Andreas, including letters she had written seeking help locating documentation about her brother. On March 26, 1995, she had written to the Netherlands Embassy:

From 1939–1947 I lived in Holland as a refugee from Hitler's Germany. My brother Andreas Fröhlich was arrested in 1941 in Amsterdam, held at Schoorl and later at Mauthausen. He was reported deceased a few months later. We received the—not unexpected—message via a friend who had checked the list at the Joodse Raad. My parents and I survived the war as onderduikers [hidden persons].

We will be in Holland in April and I am hoping to somehow get access to the archives of the Joodse Raad. I intend to visit Mauthausen on another trip and would like to make contact with any survivor or organization of survivors of Mauthausen. I have read extensively about the KZ [Konzentrationslager, concentration camp] with the help of a bibliography from the Library at the U.S. Holocaust Museum in Washington.

You may understand that the death of my brother is "unfinished business" for me. My parents have since died and no one in my family has ever seen Andreas' name on any list. His name may not even be on any Mauthausen record, but it must be listed in Amsterdam or wherever the archives are...

I am asking for your assistance in getting access to the archives in Holland, so that I may copy that record for our children and grandchildren. I also hope you can give me address/phone number of organizations which keep the memory of Mauthausen alive. They may be helpful in getting me to see the archives of Mauthausen in Austria. I had gone to the Austrian Tourist Office in New York some years ago to find railroad connections, etc. I was handed tourist pamphlets extolling "Radlerparadies" [bicycler's paradise] and listing 2 "Gedankstatten" [memorials] there as the KZ and a Kriegerfriedhof [cemetery for warriors]. You can imagine how this shocked me. Visitors to the KZ have to pay an entrance fee and I am sure that I can't expect any special treatment/access there if I just show up. I need to find a written record somewhere!

A Mr. A.J. van den Berge responded on behalf of the Netherlands embassy. In a faxed letter, dated April 3, 1995, he recommended that Mom contact the Rijksinstituut voor Oorlogsdocumentatie (RIOD) [Government Institute for War Documentation].[1] He also informed her about the Vriendenkring Mauthausen.

Two days later, Mom sent a letter to the RIOD:

> I am looking for documentation on the arrest, deportation and death of my brother **ANDREAS FROEHLICH** (or Frohlich with an Umlaut), born October 14, 1921 in Breslau, Germany. Our address at the time of the arrest was **Prins Hendriklaan 36**, Amsterdam-Zuid. I was home alone when two Dutch police (?) in plain clothes came and looked for him. As far as I can reconstruct the date, it was June 1941...

> I am very anxious to find his name on any document pertaining to his arrest, deportation and death. I have read extensively about conditions and record keeping at Mauthausen. The date and reason given for his death may be wholly fictitious.

On May 4, a Mevr. drs. A. van Bockxmeer of the RIOD responded:

> Dear Mrs. Schipper,

> I hereby send you a photocopy of a document out of the Durchgangslager Westerbork [transit camp in the Netherlands], in which there is mention that your brother Andreas Froehlich died in Mauthausen. The print is not easy to read, but it appears to state that the death date of your brother is 28 October 1941.

Enclosed was a grainy, typed list of 38 persons, alphabetized from Friedberg to Furth, with columns for last and first names, birthdate, former address and death date. Near the middle of the list is:

Froehlich loot, 14-10-21, A'dam, P.H.Laan 36, 28-10-41 Mauth. ovl.

The last name, birthdate and address matched what my mother knew. The first name, "loot" is a misspelling of Lot. Males the Nazis deemed Jews were forced to take on more "Jewish" names such as Lot. Mauth. is an abbreviation for Mauthausen and ovl., an abbreviation of *overleden* [died]. Fifty years after WWII had ended, Mom had found a document listing a specific date of death for her brother.

Ms. Bockxmeer wrote that the Westerbork camp's management had ordered that its records be destroyed during the last winter of the war. The prisoners, those who were still working in the camp administration, saw this edict coming and secretly took data from the camp records and made copies of the lists. When the Westerbork camp was liberated, the prisoners gave their lists to the Canadians, who made two further copies of them. What Mom received was a copy of the Canadian photocopy. The original Westerbork camp records were never found after the war.

Ms. Bockxmeer gave Mom the address of the Information Bureau of the Netherlands Red Cross and the address of Mrs. H. Dominicus of the Vriedenkring Mauthausen. The letter closed with, "I hope from my heart that you will succeed in finding more information about your brother. In the collection of RIOD, I found only the entry in the lists from Westerbork."

Mom contacted Mrs. Dominicus of the Vriendenkring by phone the same month, then followed up by letter in August. Mom asked how she could obtain a memorial book about Mauthausen, "because I am gathering as much as I can about the war years for my children." She described her research and her hope to join the Vriendenkring on a trip to Mauthausen in 1996. She asked whether the Archive Memorial of Mauthausen granted access to families of victims. She said she would write the Austrian Ambassador but expected little cooperation. "To complete my search, I will look up Andreas' (Lot) name on another list of Mauthausen itself."

I did not find any correspondence to or from the Austrian Embassy in Mom's folder of Mauthausen materials. Nor did I find any photocopy of a record from Mauthausen's archives with her brother's name.

Many years later, however, I would find what my mother was searching for while researching the history of the Mauthausen camp. I checked the camp's official website again and seemed to have missed the link for a "Virtual Room of Names" described as a DIGITAL MEMORIAL BOOK FOR THE DEAD OF THE MAUTHAUSEN CONCENTRATION CAMP AND ITS SUBCAMPS 1938-1945.

On that digital page, a tab opened up: "Please enter a name." So I did.

"Andreas Fröhlich."

Response: "No record found."

I tried "Andreas Froehlich." Nothing. Then I tried "Lot Fröhlich or Froehlich." And up came:

Lot Froehlich 1921–1941

Born 14.10.1921 in Breslau / Wrocław

Died 28.10.1941 in Mauthausen

There was a link under this entry marked "Biography." I clicked on it and it said, "No biography available for Lot Froehlich." But underneath that was a tab for "Send information about this person." So I did.

While I was heartened to find an entry for Andreas, I was disheartened that it was under the Nazi-imposed name of "Lot." Frankly, the discovery that the Nazi-imposed name followed Andreas to his death and beyond in the Mauthausen records infuriated me. So the information I entered on April 30, 2018 was:

His name was Andreas Fröhlich, not Lot. The Nazis stripped young men of their given names if they were deemed Jewish and assigned names such as "Lot" and "Moses" as the only names allowed for those of Jewish ancestry. Andreas was forced to be registered as Lot when he was a German refugee in the Netherlands during WWII before he was transported to and killed in Mauthausen. Seeing him listed in your records as "Lot" is one more reminder of what the Nazis did to strip people of their identity and humanity before torturing and killing them. Andreas was the son of Edith (Nissen) Fröhlich and Georg Fröhlich and the brother of Sabine G. Fröhlich. My name is Agnes Schipper and Andreas Fröhlich would have been my uncle had he been allowed to live. Andreas was raised Catholic and hoped to become a priest. I will send more biographical information later on, as I am writing a family history. I visited your camp with my mother, Sabine (Fröhlich) Schipper in 1998. Andreas' name was added to the Netherlands Monument at Mauthausen in 1996. He is correctly listed as Andreas Fröhlich on the Netherlands Monument.

Two days later, I was surprised to receive a very cordial reply by email from Katharina Kniefacz of the Mauthausen Memorial organization. She thanked me for my message via the Room of Names website and explained the history of the "Lot" Froehlich entry:

The virtual "Room of Names" was presented in 2016 and the work is still in progress. The project represents the interim conclusion to research work carried out continuously over several years to reconstruct the names and dates of those who died. Main sources are thousands of still existing SS documents, which list your uncle as "Lot (Israel) Froehlich".

Unfortunately, in many cases it was not yet possible to reconstruct the names in the original form. The ongoing additions and revisions to the list of names remain an important task for the Memorial and this project. – Therefore, we would like to thank you very much for the information of your uncle's correct name. Of course we have immediately corrected it in the "Room of Names" as well as in our database.

Ms. Kniefacz attached a query from the prisoners' database with the corrected information and a copy of a scan of a transport list documenting that Andreas "was committed to Mauthausen concentration camp on June 23, 1941, with a transport of 92 Dutch and German Jewish prisoners, who had been arrested during the raid in

Amsterdam on June 11, 1941. In Mauthausen, he was allocated prisoner number 1983. His profession was written as *Drucker* (printer) and he was categorized as a Jewish prisoner from the Netherlands."

Ms. Kniefacz also enclosed a copy of a single, handwritten line from the Mauthausen camp's death registers recording that Andreas died on October 28, 1941, at 4:30 p.m. due to *Lungenentzündung, Kreislaufschwäche* (pneumonia, circulatory weakness). About this entry she cautioned: "Please note that the given cause of death does not necessarily correlate with the actual reasons for the prisoner's demise. Often murders were disguised as 'natural cases of death.'"

Ms. Kniefacz invited me to add biographical information and photographs of Andreas, commenting that the memorial organization "would be glad to upload it and grateful for your participation in this common project!" She wrote that she unfortunately was not able to retrieve more original documents and suggested I contact the International Tracing Service of the Red Cross.

I read that email the morning of May 2 in our hotel room at the Ritz-Carlton in Sarasota. (My husband John and I had checked into the hotel the night before to celebrate our sixth wedding anniversary.) I broke down in tears as I read the email to John. I felt terrible regret that Mom had not seen the virtual "Room of Names" while she was alive. Her "unfinished business" was to see his name on war-era records and find out what she could about Andreas' "arrest, deportation and death."

Now, we have a record of his deportation. He arrived at the camp less than two weeks after he was arrested. He was already doomed, but his family did not know it. I felt anger at the Nazi bastards who sent him to that death camp. I felt immense sadness at what Andreas must have experienced in his final months.

But I also felt a small measure of vindication. As Mom wrote to the Vriendenkring in 1995, "To complete my search, I will look up Andreas' (Lot) name on another list of Mauthausen itself." No list of names was available when we visited Mauthausen in 1998. The Mauthausen Memorial added the Room of Names years after our trip there. The museum has the names of all known victims printed in a book and engraved in white on a virtual black marble tablet-like surface that fills the Room of Names.

Well, Mom, "Lot" Frohlich *is* on the lists of Mauthausen itself. But I did not want to see the anonymity of that Nazi-assigned name persist in those camp records. Andreas' real name—his birth name—will now be memorialized at the camp. I submitted a biography and pictures of him so he will be remembered as a loved human being, not just as Lot Froehlich, Prisoner No. 1983.[2]

As Ms. Kniefacz suggested, I did contact the International Tracing Service (ITS) of the Red Cross. More than a year later, on May 13, 2019, I received a 33-page trove of documents from the ITS. The very first record was a photocopy of an index card from the archives of the Joodse Raad, the Jewish Council in Amsterdam, a record that Mom had sought without success. The card had the name of "Froehlich loot," his birthdate, Prins Hendriklaan address, *Juni-groep* (June group), prisoner number and death date. This was the only record related to his arrest.

The *Juni-groep* entry raised questions for me: How was it that Andreas had been targeted for the June group roundup? Did the Jewish Council have a role in this? Did the council provide information about Andreas to the Gestapo?

The answer is yes, though the council was not told at the time that the list of names and addresses it provided to the Gestapo would be used to send young men to death camps in retaliation for an act of sabotage. The Gestapo's roundup in June focused on Jewish students in Amsterdam who were refugees from Germany.[3]

The ITS records contained more awful information. On page 7 was a handwritten notation about an "operation under anesthesia" for Lot Fröhlich on October 4, 1941. The entry *Spaltung Achseldrüsenabscess rechts* translates to "incision (or splitting) axillary abscesses right."

Also chilling is that *Spaltung* is listed on nine of the 15 surgical procedures performed on that same day.

Given the utter lack of regard for human life at the camp, why operate on an abscess under Andreas' right arm three weeks before his death? Was the abscess the result of an injury or beating? Was the procedure even carried out by a real doctor or under anesthesia? Was Andreas used for medical experiments? Did the surgery lead to his death? We know the Nazi records at Mauthausen are full of fictions to cover up atrocities and murders. All possible explanations for the operation are ghastly.

Ms. Kniefacz had forwarded a single handwritten line recording Andreas' death, but seeing that entry in the context of a full page listing all deaths for the same day better conveys the scale of the horror at Mauthausen. His was one of 12 deaths recorded for October 28, 1941, including several listed as caused by *"Freitod durch Spring in die Tiefe"* ("suicide by jumping into the depths"). Five deaths are recorded between 7:30 and 7:45, two at 7:30 and the next three exactly five minutes apart.

Lot Fröhlich's death is inserted among ten deaths listed for October 29, so obviously postdated. Even the officially recorded date and time of death are suspect. You cannot help but get the sense that whoever was documenting these deaths was not only assigning an arbitrary time and date, but also was selecting the manner of death from a Nazi-approved list of causes—more reinforcement that the records for all these poor young men were nothing but a bundle of cynical lies. Hard to read without feeling immense pity for the victims and revulsion for their tormentors.

The ITS documents included several typed pages from the *Sterbebuch* (the Book of the Deceased) at Mauthausen for 1941. The *Sterbebuch* has a list of abbreviations for religions of the deceased including "rk" for *Romish-Katholisch* (Roman Catholic), *"eve"* for *"evangelisch"* (Protestant) and *"mos"* for *"mosaisch"* or Mosaic faith, i.e. Jewish. Lot Fröhlich is on the list, with a notation of *"mos."* Another cruel irony of mislabeling; by religion, Andreas was a Roman Catholic.

The surgery on Andreas referenced earlier is also listed in a "Certificate of Incarceration" issued by the International Red Cross on February 2, 1966. The certificate was prepared at the request of Bruno Sonnabend, a lawyer who worked in my grandfather's law firm in Breslau and who reconnected with Georg after the war. In his initial correspondence with the Red Cross in 1965, Mr. Sonnabend noted that the Fröhlichs did not know the exact date of Andreas' death in Mauthausen.

Mr. Sonnabend might have sought the certificate of incarceration with a death date as required proof for a compensation claim filed on behalf of the Fröhlichs. Perhaps the request was just to help them learn more about the fate of their son. I have no-one to ask. I do not know what information Mr. Sonnabend shared with my grandparents. But I do know that this information from ITS was *not* shared with Mom—perhaps a well-meant effort to shield her from the full horror of it all?

Mom did send a request to the US Holocaust Memorial Museum in 2008 for any records about Andreas from the then newly opened and digitized archives of the ITS. However, her request was for documents pertaining to *Andreas* Fröhlich, not the Nazi assigned name of Lot, or its misspelled version, Loot. As far as I know, she did not receive any documents because the ITS records from Mauthausen are all under the name Lot.

We now have the records with her brother's name that Mom had searched for "to copy for our children and grandchildren."

In 2021, four years after Mom's death, the Mauthausen Memorial published a book titled "*...and the Block was Jew-free*" *The Nazi Persecution of Jews in the Netherlands and their murder in the Mauthausen* *concentration camp.* The book, in German, includes the last photograph taken of Andreas and the story of his arrest and death in Mauthausen.[4]

A Stolperstein in memory of Andreas will be placed in front of Prins Hendriklaan 36 and 38 in May 2022.

3

MAUTHAUSEN CONCENTRATION CAMP

Mom's Research on Mauthausen

My mother created small library of reference materials on the Mauthausen concentration camp and wrote many pages of notes of her research. I try to imagine her poring through bibliographies at the US Holocaust Memorial Museum in Washington, D.C, and reading books, pamphlets, whatever she could gather about this god-awful camp. Her research predated modern search engines such as Google. She was on a tenacious mission to find out all she could about Mauthausen and her brother's "arrest, deportation and death."

Mom confronted the task of her "unfinished business" with unrelenting persistence. Stubbornness was a character trait for her. Some might have flinched after reading a few gruesome accounts about Mauthausen and not had the stomach or fortitude to continue to read more about that terrible time and place. Not Mom. She searched on, despite accepting the reality from the outset that she might never learn exactly what happened to her brother.

One of her binders contained photocopied bibliographies and pages from books about Mauthausen that I have used in writing this chapter. She also collected the Austrian government's official guide to the "Public Memorial and Museum Mauthausen," published in 1996 and the guidebook we used when we visited the camp in 1998.[1] Mom marked an "X" next to only three passages and underlined only one sentence in that 32-page booklet. I will highlight those because I have to assume those notations identify the information she found particularly pertinent to her brother's imprisonment.

This chapter will be hard to read, but I feel it is important to learn and not forget the history of the Mauthausen camp, the hideousness of Nazism and the sheer cruelty the human mind is capable of conceiving and inflicting. Knowing the history helps gives context when you visit the remnants of a camp decades after it was liberated.

The Quarry

Mauthausen is not as well-known a concentration camp as, for example, Auschwitz. Located in upper Austria, the town of Mauthausen is on the Danube River, about 13 miles southeast of the city of Linz where Hitler spent his youth. Before WWII, Mauthausen was known in Austria for its granite quarries. The City of Vienna owned several quarries (*Weiner Graben*) in the area and used them to supply paving stones for its streets.

Hitler had grand architectural plans to transform the small city of Linz into a *Führerstadt* (Führer city), designated to become the cultural center of the Third Reich. The monumental building schemes included an Olympic stadium, an observatory, new municipal buildings, Wehrmacht headquarters, Hitler's retirement home, a hall and tower for his crypt and the Führermuseum, to contain the largest, most comprehensive painting collection in Europe.

High output from quarries was needed for Hitler's grandiose and massive building schemes. Early on in the Third Reich, the Nazi SS (*Schutzstaffel*) planned on building concentration camps in mining areas and using camp prisoners as cheap labor to work in those quarries. The SS was paramilitary organization of the Nazi party charged with security, surveillance, and enforcement of Nazi racial policies and management of concentration camps.

In May 1938, a few weeks after German troops occupied Austria, Heinrich Himmler and Oswald Pohl, two high ranking SS officers, visited the Mauthausen quarry. They decided it was a suitable location for a concentration camp and the Vienna municipality leased its three quarries to the SS for a period of 10 years.[2]

On August 8, 1938, the first prisoners were transferred from the Dachau concentration camp to begin construction of a concentration camp high on a hill above the town of Mauthausen. The Mauthausen camp became the central concentration camp for Austria, and the administrative center for its 49 subcamps. The camp guards were SS men who referred to Mauthausen as the "mother camp." The SS attracted the worst of humanity: sadists, psychopaths, sociopaths, terrorists and mass murderers.

Mauthausen's Camp Classification

My mother's first "X" is on page 7 in the guidebook alongside the following sentence: In addition, there were a small number of Austrian and German prisoners serving prison sentences for criminal offences [sic], who fulfilled almost all supervisory functions in the camp until the spring of 1944.

In other words, known criminal sociopaths were the overlords, called kapos, at the camp.

Another "X" was next to the following on page 19:

> Decree by R. Heydrich, Head of Security Police and Security Service (January 2, 1941), introducing the following classification of concentration camps: [...] Stage III ... the Mauthausen camp for particularly severe cases, including persons with a criminal record and anti-social elements, i.e. person in preventive detention unlikely to respond to re-education.

This classification, worse than the Stage or Category II assigned to Buchenwald and Auschwitz, is significant in explaining the particularly brutal conditions at Mauthausen. As one writer summarized:

> Only Mauthausen received the harshest classification. Mauthausen was intended only for prisoners "for whom there was no prospect of being brought back into the fold"; this meant that the transfer of a prisoner to Mauthausen was tantamount to a death sentence. Even when the camp was first built, work in the Mauthausen quarry was carried out by the most primitive and brutal methods, which led to the death of prisoners in a very short space of time.[3]

Gusen Subcamp

About three miles from Mauthausen was Gusen, a quarry that an SS-owned stoneworks firm purchased in 1938. Guards initially marched contingents of prisoners back and forth from Mauthausen to work at the Gusen quarry. In 1939, the SS authorized construction of a concentration camp in Gusen, saving the work time lost during the daily marches.

The Mauthausen Memorial website describes the two quarries:

> The Mauthausen and Gusen quarries were sites of forced labor and places of annihilation in equal measure. While, on the one hand, there was a permanent shortage of skilled labor in the quarries, on the other hand the prisoners were systematically worked to death. Back-breaking work as punishment and deliberate killing operations were part of everyday life....

> The grueling work and inadequate food rations drained prisoners' strength and left them emaciated. Working without proper equipment led to any number of injuries. Close quarters in the barracks and a lack of hygiene in the camp fostered the spread of infectious diseases.[4]

First Political Prisoners arrive in 1939; Executions begin

From the beginning of the war, the SS and German police used the concentration camps as execution sites for political opponents. This applied in particular measure to the Mauthausen and Gusen concentration camps; many prisoners were deported to these camps simply for execution.

The first political prisoners who arrived at the camp in 1939 were communists and socialists from Czechoslovakia. In 1940, 300 Roma (Gypsies) were transferred there along with thousands of Poles and Spanish Republicans, including children and adolescents. Subsequently, train loads of Poles and Czechs, many of them artists, intellectuals and priests, arrived, as well as prisoners from Yugoslavia. Even later, thousands of prisoners of war from the Soviet Union were sent to the camp.

Once delivered to the Mauthausen concentration camp, prisoners were stripped of their identities. Their names were replaced with prisoner numbers. They wore colored triangles on their striped prison clothing, each color indicating why they had been imprisoned. Those deemed "political" prisoners, a category that included Jews, wore a red triangle. In addition, Jews had to wear a Yellow Star of David below the red triangle. The prisoner's number was printed in black on white above, below or beside the triangle. As the Mauthausen Memorial website explains: "Each category was linked to the degree of terror used by the SS, better or worse accommodation, or the prospect of a privileged post in the camp organisation (sic). Those marked as 'Jews' had the lowest chances of survival."[5]

Dutch Prisoners arrive in 1941

In February 1941, the Dutch staged a general strike to protest the treatment of Jews. In response, Himmler ordered a *razzia*, rounding up 389 Jewish men as hostages who were sent to Buchenwald. Some perished in Buchenwald, while others were transferred to

23

Mauthausen at the beginning of the summer. On June 11, in retaliation for an act of sabotage, the Gestapo staged a second *razzia* in Amsterdam, arresting another 276 young men of Jewish ancestry. In all, the arrival of 900 Dutch Jews to Mauthausen was recorded in 1941. No more than eight survived to the end of the year, and not one lived to see liberation.[6]

Andreas was rounded up in the second razzia. Although apolitical and a practicing Catholic, he nevertheless, would have been classified as a "political" prisoner and been forced to wear a red triangle superimposed on a yellow Star of David, and his prison number 1983 marked on his clothing —his identity officially obliterated. Even being categorized as a prisoner sounds wrong: Andreas was a hostage; there was no legal or rational basis for his arrest and imprisonment.

The Death Steps

Mauthausen is notorious for its *Todessteige* (death steps or stairs of death), a term used for the 186 steps that led to and from the quarry. The official guidebook notes that the steps were constructed in 1942. Before that time, the steps had been formed by randomly selected and loosely placed rocks and boulders of unequal size.[7]

As to Jewish prisoners at Mauthausen from Holland, the historian Dr. Eugene Kogon wrote that they "were not allowed to walk [down] the 148 steps [Mom wrote in a correction: 186 steps] that led to the depths [of the quarry] but had to slide down a slope of small loose stones, causing many deaths and severe injuries."[8]

Prisoners were forced to climb back up the steps while carrying blocks of granite weighing up to 50kg on a wooden frame harnessed to their backs for 11 hours a day. The Nazis named the camp *Knochenschleifer* (the bone grinder). One picture shows hundreds of inmates, five across per step, carrying those blocks on their backs. The march up the quarry steps was accompanied by beatings from the guards. Exhausted prisoners would often collapse and topple back on those following them, creating a domino effect of crushed bodies.

"Parachutists"

Mauthausen was also notorious for its *Fallschirmspringer Klippe* (Parachutists' Cliff). The SS guards gave the cynical name of "parachutists" to the prisoners who fell to their deaths from the cliffs above the quarry. The literature about Mauthausen is consistent and specific that many of the Dutch prisoners were singled out for this torture.

The only passage my mother underlined in the Austrian guidebook is on page 15:

> Prisoners were pushed off the steep face of the quarry between the approach road and the death steps by SS guards. <u>Entire groups of Dutch Jews were killed that way</u>. That is why the guards referred to the place as parachutists' cliff.

Such deaths were recorded in official camp documents as "suicide by jumping."

Accounts about the "parachutists" differ, with some saying these included suicides by Jewish prisoners who linked hands and jumped to their deaths. Other accounts disagree, claiming guards forced the prisoners over the brink of the quarry. In the book *The 186 Steps,* the author Christian Bernadac, quotes Alois Höllriegl, a Mauthausen guard who testified at the Nuremberg trials:

> From the guard watchtower I saw two SS guards who were striking the prisoners, and was able to note that they wanted to force them to leap over the cliff, or else they pushed them. I saw one prisoner, lying on the ground, who was stomped on. Their gestures showed that they were ordering him to jump off the cliff. Finally the prisoner did so, probably out of despair because of all the blows he had already received.[9]

Whether the "parachutists" were forced to jump or some jumped themselves out of desperation is ultimately irrelevant. It's all murder. Jumping was not voluntary, whether done at gunpoint, pushed by guards or because of unbearable conditions.

Crematoria and Execution Rooms

In 1940, due to the rising number of prisoner deaths, the SS had incinerators installed at both Mauthausen and the nearby camp of Gusen, and later at the Melk and Ebensee subcamps. Adjacent to one of the cremation furnaces in Mauthausen was the "dissecting room" where gold teeth were broken out of corpses' mouths.

An apparatus for shooting prisoners in the back of the neck was installed in the basement near the crematorium. As a ruse, a camera or a device for height measurements would be set up in the basement room. The prisoner would be told to stand against a wall to be photographed or directed to the corner to stand in front of the measuring device. A SS man behind the wall then would shoot the prisoner through holes bored in the wall or through a slot in the measuring device's headboard. Afterwards, an inmate would enter the room quickly to drag away the body and wipe away any traces of the slaughter before the next victim was summoned. This method was used to kill inmates individually at a rate of about one every two minutes, or 30 per hour. Prisoners were also executed by hanging in the room that held the oil furnace for the crematorium.[10]

On the north slope outside the camp was the "Ash Pile" where the remains of cremated bodies were dumped. As the prisoner population and slaughter increased, three crematoria were constructed within the boundaries of the Mauthausen camp.

Neglect and Murder of the Sick, Gas Chambers

In early 1941, the SS began *Aktion 14f13*, a centrally planned killing operation for weak and sick concentration camp prisoners. The first gassing chamber was built at the nearby Castle Hartheim. Starting in August 1941, panels of doctors selected those who were seriously ill from the Gusen and Mauthausen concentration camps and transported them to the Hartheim killing facility near Linz. The prisoners were usually asphyxiated in the gas chamber shortly after their arrival and their bodies were then burned in the crematorium there. Smoke and stench belched from the castle, tufts of human hair flew from the chimney onto the street, and pieces of unground bone fell off trucks taking the ashes and cremation residue from the castle to be dumped in the Danube River.[11]

Around 5,000 prisoners from Mauthausen and Gusen were gassed in Hartheim as part of Aktion 14f13. In the autumn of 1941, construction began on a gas chamber in Mauthausen and, in March 1942, the SS carried out the first murders there using Xyklon B poison gas. The first victims of the gas chamber were Soviet prisoners of war who had been transferred from Wehrmacht camps to the Mauthausen concentration camp for execution. By the end of the war, at least 3,500 inmates had been murdered in the gas chamber at Mauthausen.

Only a few privileged inmates received adequate medical care in what was known as the infirmary. There the prisoners were treated mainly by doctors and orderlies who were also inmates. Prisoners who had become unfit for work through illness were seen as useless by the SS; hardly any medical care was provided for them. They were mistreated by SS doctors for medical experiments, murdered by poison injection or in the gas chamber, or left to their own devices in isolated areas of the camp. In an area separated off within the prisoner camp, the sick were left to die or their death was hastened through decreasing rations.[12]

Mom's handwritten research notes include accounts (in German) of typhoid outbreaks in the camp during the summer of 1941 while Andreas was imprisoned there. We now know that Andreas was operated on a few weeks before his death. What we do not know and will never know is the real cause of his death—whether he was neglected and left to die afterwards,

murdered by poison injection, gassed in Hartheim Castle as part of Aktion
14f13 *or killed by some other gruesome method. For the families of victims in
Mauthausen, it's hard to contemplate which is worse: knowing or not
knowing.*

Camps and the local populace

The Mauthausen camp employed civilians from local towns, and also
brought business to local tradesmen and artisans who delivered
goods and provided services at the camp. From the beginning,
Mauthausen residents witnessed how SS guards treated prisoners
when they arrived at the local train station (2.5 miles from the camp)
and as they were being marched to work sites.

One Mauthausen resident spoke of having seen a group of
"beautifully dressed" Dutch Jews with suitcases, walking from the
train station, one struggling with his luggage. She implored them to
drop their belongings and spare themselves the burden because
everything would be taken away anyway when they reached the
camp. An SS guard shouted at her and the captives were unable to let
go of their belongings.[13]

As time passed, the civil population was increasingly exposed to the
sight of mistreatment, brutalization and murder of inmates. A
resident who lived within view of the Mauthausen camp quarry
witnessed inmates being shot and others being struck down by
guards and left for hours alongside the dead. She filed a complaint in
1941 with the local police department, stating that she was sickly, and
that witnessing "such outrages" was unbearable for her nerves. She
requested that "it be arranged that such inhuman deeds be
discontinued, or else be done where one does not see it." Though
cognizant of the terror at the camps, the local residents "learned to
walk a narrow line between unavoidable awareness and prudent
disregard," as one author described the mentality."[14]

Mauthausen's Reputation as a Death Camp, 1942–1945

By 1942, Mauthausen had the grim reputation of a death sentence in the Netherlands. Between 1942 and 1944 the Nazis transported political prisoners en masse to Mauthausen from all over Europe, as well as sending thousands of unregistered Soviet prisoners of war there. In these later years, slave laborers were sent from Mauthausen and its subcamps to construct armaments factories in the nearby mountains. In 1945, more than 20,000 prisoners from concentration camps in countries ceded by the Germans were transferred to Mauthausen, from Lublin, Auschwitz and other camps. At the same time, thousands of Hungarian civilians—mostly Jews—were delivered to the camp.

Liberation

Mauthausen was the last concentration camp liberated. In the face of the advancing Allied troops, in April 1945 the SS began to destroy the traces of its crimes. The SS dismantled installations for mass killing, ordered incriminating documents to be burned, and murdered concentration camp prisoners who, having witnessed systematic mass murder first-hand, would have been able to testify against the perpetrators in court.

On May 3, 1945 the last members of the SS fled the Mauthausen and Gusen concentration camps. On May 5, a reconnaissance unit of the US Army arrived in Gusen and Mauthausen. On the following day, units of the 3rd US Army finally liberated the prisoners in these camps.

In both camps, soldiers found the bodies of hundreds of prisoners who had died in the days before liberation. Thousands more were so weak and their health so frail that they died in the weeks and months following liberation, despite the care provided by the US Army medical units. Over 3,000 of these victims were buried in "Camp Cemeteries" next to the former concentration camps.

A "War Crimes Investigating Team" also arrived in Mauthausen together with the US troops. The team collected evidence of SS war crimes—including key SS documents, which the prisoners had rescued from destruction at risk to their own lives—and in doing so created the basis for the legal prosecution of the perpetrators.[15]

Mauthausen, the Unknown Toll

The final thing to understand about Mauthausen is that we will never know the full truth about the camp. We will never know exactly how many people were imprisoned, tortured and perished there, nor the actual cause of death for most of its victims.

Despite the Nazi stereotype for meticulous documentation, unreliable record-keeping and statistics were a pattern from Mauthausen's earliest days. Evelyn Le Chêne, a French Resistance member who was imprisoned in Mauthausen and survived, wrote about the wide discrepancies and under-reporting of prisoner numbers by the Nazis. "It is obvious that the significant lapse in the registration of incoming prisoners between 1940 and 1942 were part of the overall plan of extermination of the Jews."[16]

This pattern persisted to the camp's last days. When Americans liberated the camp on May 3, 1945, "a total of 64,800 men and 1,784 women were officially registered as inmates of the Mauthausen concentration camp, in addition to some 15,000 non-registered prisoners." Because official figures are incomplete and unreliable, estimates are that between 90,000 and 110,000 prisoners were killed or died because of the atrocious conditions at Mauthausen and its subcamps.[17]

Hitler's grand building plans for Linz were never realized.

4

PILGRIMAGE TO MAUTHAUSEN, 1998

For health reasons, my mother could not make the trip to Mauthausen in 1996, the year when the Vriendenkring had Andreas' name added to the Netherlands Monument. The following year, 1997, was the year of my parents' 50th wedding anniversary. Mom was preoccupied with organizing a reunion for the entire family—five children, their spouses or significant others, and 12 grandchildren—in the Netherlands for a weeklong celebration. But by 1998, she was ready and felt physically able to join the Vriendenkring on its annual journey from Amsterdam to Mauthausen.

Mom invited me to join her on the trip and I accepted without hesitation. Her binder on Mauthausen included her emails to me about the trip. On 1/23/98, she wrote:

> Agnes, I am going with a group, who all have lost friends or relatives at M[authausen]. It is not an occasion for a family reunion... I have waited many years to make this trip and I need peace of mind, most of all. You have always said you would come along, and I am happy about that. After all, you are or will be the family historian!

On 1/25/98, another email:

...Try to get the book by Evelyn Le Chêne: the 186 steps, inter library loan or any college of university with a Holocaust program. Then you will know what happened there before you see it. I have read almost everything about M., had a printout from the H.[olocaust] Museum and of course, bibliographies lead to more books. We can talk about it on the train trip.

I came from Minnesota to Philadelphia to join Mom on her flight to Amsterdam. Traveling became increasingly difficult and strenuous because of her decreasing lung capacity and weak bones, the lifetime toll of asthma treated with steroid medication. The long corridors and stairs at many airports were daunting. In 1997 for the 50th anniversary celebration, she traveled to Amsterdam via Heathrow and swore off ever transferring through that airport again. She managed to climb down the stairs off the plane at Heathrow, but became breathless when she had to climb back up stairs inside the terminal. Her hip must have begun to disintegrate back in 1998. Within a few years, she would need to use a wheelchair to travel, then have to have a hip replacement.

Mom planned to spend a few days in Amsterdam before beginning the train trip to Austria. She arranged a luncheon at a restaurant with former classmates from her Catholic high school days. She was an avid correspondent who had kept in touch with many of her Dutch friends for decades after she had emigrated to the United States.

I remember the dim room at the restaurant, with dark wood paneling, tall stained-glass windows and high ceilings. Very old-world Dutch. She and her friends talked and laughed non-stop. I remember taking photographs and videotaping at the restaurant, but don't know what happened to those videos and pictures, perhaps another casualty of my multiple moves. I have not yet found these photos in my mother's effects—and she was a pack-rat. I'm guessing she sent the photos to her Dutch friends.

Before we began the train trip, we met with the group organized by the Vriendenkring that would be traveling to Mauthausen. The group included Ies, one of the few who survived Mauthausen, and his wife, Esther. Ies was 12 when he was sent to Auschwitz. He was transferred to Mauthausen near the end of the war, spending four months there before being liberated.

Two of the group had lost brothers at Mauthausen; one, her father, only a few months before liberation. Fietje, a heavy set elderly woman who hobbled with a cane, had lost her father, brother and a nephew. Most relatives of the victims came with their spouses and many with their grown children, as my mother did. All brought together by a common bond of loss, and by a desire to share that history with the next generation. A Dutch lawyer and historian and two psychiatry students joined the group, making up a total of about 28.

In the course of that week, these people became like family. I was so grateful that my mother could make that journey with a supportive group that could understand her need for closure. In the course of that rail trip to and from Mauthausen, I interviewed Mom and learned much of her family's history for the first time. It was a rare and precious time we had together on those smooth European rails: no competing siblings, no kids to placate, no phones to answer, meals to cook, briefs to write—no distractions. I took copious notes in a green notebook and placed them in a turquoise plastic envelope, to be typed up later.

After a long train ride, we boarded a bus for the final leg to Mauthausen, stopping along the way to buy flowers to lay at the Netherlands' monument to victims of the concentration camp. At the flower shop, I burst into tears.

I had expected to approach a camp that looked like the pictures I had seen about Auschwitz: grim, gray, dreary, industrial looking. Instead, we were traveling through a beautiful landscape. Rolling hills covered with grass and flowers, sunshine and clear, blue skies; picture-postcard pretty. As advertised, Mauthausen was a "bicycler's paradise." And here, on the high slopes above the Danube River, with a panoramic view of the lovely Austrian countryside, the Nazis had built a fortress to enslave, torture and murder innocents. Here in paradise they created a living hell. The dissonance was so jarring, I felt physically ill.

As the bus climbed up the hill and approached the camp entrance, the foreboding darkness of the place came into view. Hulking watch towers, high stone walls. Large wooden entrance doors opening directly into the *Appellplatz* (roll call plaza), a massive open cobblestoned courtyard, an assembly place where thousands of emaciated prisoners had to stand for hours in freezing temperatures. A place where they were forced to watch executions.

It was hard to grasp the true enormity of the evil, cruelty, barbarism and depravity of this place by walking through its remnants 50 years later. As the opening paragraph of the Austrian government's official guidebook to the camp states:

> From 1938–1945, Mauthausen was a name that spread fear and terror. Mauthausen-Gusen was synonymous with death through slave labor in the quarries. ... The soil of this vast stronghold is soaked with the blood of thousands of innocent people.

More accurately, it should say tens of thousands of innocents. The guidebook on Mauthausen has a fold-out map of the camp on the inside of the back cover. Black rectangles and squares on the map reflect "still existing objects." Pale gray rectangles on the map presumably reflect "no longer existing objects." Most of the 30-plus "huts," cell blocks into which the prisoners were crammed under terrible conditions, are rendered in gray—gone.

On the right side of the Appellplatz, adjacent to the camp walls, the map shows a row of buildings in black, and, in order from the entrance gate, they are labeled: kitchen, laundry, camp jail, crematorium, gas chamber, execution corner and sick quarters (now museum).

In the guidebook, Mom had written an "X" next to the description for Hut 5, a gray rectangle adjacent to a barbed wire fence at the back of the camp on the map. Hut 5 is labeled: Sick quarters and Jewish block. Almost all of the 2,700 to 2,800 Jewish political prisoners housed in Section B of the last hut of the first row between 1941 and March 1944 were put to death. The sick quarters were accommodated on the left side (Section A) of the hut.

Where Andreas likely spent his last days is gone; just three of 21 wooden barracks inside the main camp survive.

As we walked through the grounds on a warm, sunny spring day, it was hard to visualize this place overcrowded with slave laborers as it once had been. But grisly pictures of the camp survive to provide visual evidence of what happened here, despite Nazi attempts to destroy documentation of what they perpetrated on these grounds. Pictures of skeletal people, barely alive, sunken eyes, heads appearing disproportionate to emaciated torsos, every rib visible, legs and arms like sticks. Prisoners jammed in the Appellplatz for roll call. Bodies of prisoners in striped uniforms splayed on the ground, supposedly shot while trying to flee. A dead body bent in a jackknife dive over the top of an electrified barbed wire fence. Piles of naked corpses. SS commanders in uniforms inspecting the camp, strolling and chatting —as though they were on a pleasant, spring-time field trip.[1]

We saw the notorious death steps, now smoothed out and evenly placed for tourists to climb. We knew Andreas was here in 1941, before any real steps were built; he would have had to ascend "randomly selected and loosely placed rocks and boulders of unequal size."

We saw the parachutists' cliff, the steep drop from the top of the quarry to the base. The cliff now overlooks a small lake and grassy field. Trees and bushes have taken root in crevices of the cliff. Were it not for pictures taken in the 1940s of rows of prisoners in striped uniforms trudging up those steps with large granite blocks latched to their backs it would be hard to visualize the cliff as a site of brutality, horror and desperation. It would be hard to see the quarry's base as a repository of crushed bodies. A killing ground.

Mom spent a long time in the Mauthausen Museum ("former sick quarters"), looking closely at the displays about the history of the Mauthausen camp and reading all the explanatory information. I left the museum first and waited for her outside. When she emerged, her face was so pale she appeared almost sheet-white. I had never seen her like that and was very worried for her. "Are you okay? What happened in there?" I asked her.

"That museum exhibit said the Austrians were the first victims of Hitler and the Nazis," she answered. "First victims! How could they say that? How dare they! The Austrians welcomed Hitler with open arms. They cheered him in the streets."

I had never seen my mother white with rage. She was incensed by the revisionist history, offended by the sanitized portrayal of Austrians during the Third Reich. She felt the museum was propagating outright lies about Austria's complicity in the war.

Other impressions from Mauthausen. The extreme sadism took so many forms. The grounds have a monument to Lt. Gen. Dmitry Mikhailovich Karbyshev, a Soviet POW who was forced to stand naked outside all night in February 1945 while cold water was poured over him. He became encased in a block of ice and froze to death. Estimates vary, but between 200 to 500 other Soviet POWs were similarly murdered after attempting to escape from other POW camps.[2] Torture by ice was featured in Dante's ninth circle of hell, but not even Dante could have conjured up some of the other tortures inflicted in Mauthausen.

Mauthausen claimed victims from virtually every European nation. The camp has a wall with commemorative plaques known as the wailing wall. This is where prisoners had to wait for hours, some shackled to the wall, upon their arrival in the camp and for roll call. The Netherlands War Graves Foundation had fixed a memorial plaque to this wall recording that:

ON THE 6TH AND 7TH SEPTEMBER 1944
40 DUTCH AND 7 BRITISH SPECIAL AGENTS

WHO HAD BEEN DROPPED ABOVE GERMAN-OCCUPIED
TERRITORY
CRUELLY WERE PUT TO DEATH IN THIS CAMP BY THE NAZIS.
THEIR BODIES WERE BURNED IN THE CREMATORIUM.
AT THE RISK OF THEIR LIVES
YUGOSLAV AND RUSSIAN PRISONERS
BURIED THE ASHES OF THESE WAR-HEROES
AT THIS PLACE.

We would return to this site again during the International Memorial Day.

In 1998, more than 50 years after the camp had been liberated, memorials were still being dedicated. We were present at the former subcamp of Melk when the Dutch ambassador unveiled a memorial plaque to its Dutch victims. Thousands of slave laborers were sent to the Melk subcamp to help build tunnels in the Austrian hills to house and protect German armament factories. Most laborers died under brutal conditions.

All that is left of the Melk camp is a few rooms, including a crematorium and a room with a raised concrete slab where gold teeth were extracted from the bodies of victims. I will never forget the scream of Fietje when she entered the Melk subcamp. She said she felt the presence of her dead brother there. She spoke to her dead relatives, telling them that they will never be forgotten, and she placed a bouquet of flowers below the new memorial plaque.

The highlight of the visit to Mauthausen for Mom was the beautiful, simple ceremony at sunset on Friday, May 8, at the Netherlands Monument in the main camp of Mauthausen. There, in the company and comfort of the Vriendenkring, Mom laid flowers in honor of her brother. She touched her brother's name on the memorial. She was quiet and stoic. I don't remember her crying during the ceremony. I certainly did, watching her.

The ceremony brought her a measure of peace; it meant Andreas' existence and passing had been formally acknowledged. Andreas' remains have vanished. If he was cremated, perhaps there is some trace of him somewhere in the hills of Austria. But Mom was reassured that Andreas is no longer an anonymous victim of the Holocaust; his name is etched on a public monument. Andreas did not vanish unnoticed from this earth; he is not forgotten.

It was important ("unfinished business") for Mom to see where her brother spent his last days and to know that he would be remembered. Now, finally, she could say goodbye to him in a formal way, as a substitute for a funeral that had never taken place.

Of all the countless cruelties of the Nazis, I had not fully comprehended this one: the lack of a funeral, an occasion where relatives and friends can gather to share their memories of a person and to formally say farewell. A funeral is a rite that exists in all cultures throughout the world, throughout history. So many, many millions were deprived of this basic, universal rite during WWII.

Another lesson—although the war had ended more than 50 years earlier, for many the pain, grief and uncertainty persist. Although she had read nearly everything available about what had taken place at Mauthausen, Mom would never know exactly how her brother had died. She told me she was grateful her parents had died without ever visiting the camp or knowing how truly barbarous the conditions were there.

My grandmother Edith had Andreas' name added to the gravestone of my grandfather Georg. That gravestone is in a cemetery high in the hills of the Black Forest, outside the town of Bühlertal where the Fröhlichs spent their summers. Cemetery in German is *Friedhof*, literally translated as peace (*Frieden*) and yard (*Hof*). The cemetery is indeed a beautiful, peaceful place, lined with curvilinear rows of carefully tended plots.

When I visited the graveyard in 2008, the place was filled with blooming flowers and plants. After my grandfather died in 1971, my grandmother made weekly visits to the cemetery when she lived in the Black Forest. She rested on a nearby bench. It gave her comfort to be there. I do wonder whether future generations will visit the cemetery or maintain the private plot. Probably not. I have more confidence that Andreas' name etched in the Netherlands Monument at Mauthausen will last.

Sunday, May 10, dawned warm and sunny. It was International Memorial Day at Mauthausen, with ceremonies in the Appellplatz and at memorials erected by 19 nations whose citizens had been enslaved and murdered at Mauthausen and its subcamps. Relatives of victims traveled from all over Europe to attend the ceremonies.

I remember vividly one old gentleman walking among the memorials. He had thick white hair and white stubble on his chin. He was short, bent and bow-legged, his tan visage creased with deep wrinkles. Tears streamed down his face. Pinned on his shirt was a small Italian flag and a photograph of a dark-haired young man, presumably a family member, maybe his brother. He looked at me through his tears and pointed to the photograph on his chest. Words were not necessary to communicate his pain and sorrow. Wounds that last a lifetime.

The ceremonies for us began with members of the Vriendenkring, along with ambassadors from the Netherlands and England, placing flowers at the plaque along the wailing wall where the remains of the executed Dutch and British special agents were buried.

These victims, known as *Englandspiel slachtoffers* were Allied agents caught in German occupied territory. *Englandspiel* (England-game) was a German counterintelligence operation against Britain. *Slachtoffers* is Dutch for victims. The Dutch and English agents, trained in Britain to carry out sabotage, were unwittingly parachuted into the waiting arms of the German enemy who had penetrated the Resistance intelligence network in the Netherlands from 1942 to 1944. The intelligence compromise also resulted in the shooting down of several RAF aircraft during agent-dropping missions and the loss of vast quantities of weapons destined for the Dutch Resistance.

Controversy persists over why the British intelligence service ignored warnings that the Dutch intelligence network had been infiltrated. This England-game history made me shudder—for personal reasons. My father was a member of the Dutch Resistance who helped coordinate weapon drop missions by Allied pilots over the farm fields of North Holland.

After flowers were placed for the Dutch and British special agents, the Dutch contingent proceeded down the former death stairs to place flowers at a memorial for the "Parachutists." We then walked back up the stairs for a ceremony to place wreaths at the Netherlands Memorial. In the middle of the ceremony, which was occurring simultaneously with events at other nearby national memorials, a bicyclist swerved around the crowds and peddled through the gravel in front of the Netherlands Monument. He came within inches of hitting some of us.

So the Mauthausen grounds are part of the "bicycler's paradise" even on an international memorial day? I asked myself why the Austrians could not suspend their *Radlers Paradis* promotion for one day while relatives from all over Europe gathered to commemorate victims of a hell on earth.

After the individual national memorial ceremonies, delegations gathered together at the Appellplatz and laid more wreaths. An Austrian cardinal addressed the crowd, as did the President of Austria, who acknowledged Austrian passivity and complicity in the Holocaust. There were no shady spots, nor tents erected to help shield people from the sun. The heat was difficult to bear for older visitors, several of whom had to leave before the speeches were over. My memories of that day include the sight of the oldest Vriendenkring traveler, Leendert de Pechter, 85, a tall man, his white hair neatly combed back, in jacket and tie, traversing the death stairs and later sitting stoically through the heat to hear all the speeches at the Appellplatz. He lost a brother to Mauthausen.

The night after these ceremonies, the Vriendenkring travelers came together on a patio outside our hotel to thank the organizers of the trip who had made the newcomers feel welcomed into the circle. Despite the sadness that had brought us together, there was a lot of laughter that night as people told stories and jokes.

The next morning, we went to the train station for the trip back to Amsterdam. I planned to buy newspapers at a concession stand inside the station. Surely, the newspapers would have some stories about the events at the Mauthausen Memorial. Perhaps I would find summaries of the speeches by dignitaries. Plus, 1998 was the first year of a new Austrian national holiday in honor of war victims. Yet I had difficulty locating any newspapers with stories about the events at the Mauthausen camp the previous day. When I asked the store clerk about this, she responded that there was no coverage because the event was *nichts besonderes* (nothing special).

I wish I could write that the pilgrimage to Mauthausen brought my mother the peace of mind she sought; that her "unfinished business" had finally been concluded. It was an important journey and brought her some closure, a brief balm for a life-long loss. Near the end of her life, at age 90, she had hallucinations that her brother had escaped the Nazis in Holland and had survived, and that he was now looking for her. She became distraught that she had grown so old that he would no longer be able to recognize and find her. We tried to reason with her to calm her anxiety. Because of her increasing dementia, it was hard to convince her that Andreas had not survived.

5

GEORG FRÖHLICH AND EDITH NISSEN

On a mild spring day in 1915, a young German military officer approaches the Nissen'sche chirurgische Klinik on the corner of Winterfeldt and Blücherstrasse in Neisse, Germany. Located near the Czech border, Neisse is one of the oldest towns in the Silesia area, situated along the Neisse River, downstream from the larger Oder River. The picturesque town is surrounded by farmland and green, rolling hills.

The Nissen surgical clinic is an imposing edifice, four stories high above the ground floor, with Moorish and Gothic architectural features. The building's masonry is carefully finished and stylistically articulated. Two levels of terracotta balconies with quatrefoil openings jut out above the ample double front doors. Decorative elements adorning the facade include gothic arches framing the upper windows and parapets along the roofline. The Nissen family lives on the first story above the ground floor; the clinic, hospital and servants' quarters are on the upper floors.

Georg, the young officer, has just turned 30. He is tall, his short, straight dark brown hair parted slightly to the left and his mustache neatly trimmed. He wears pince-nez glasses to correct his nearsighted brown eyes. Georg has come to Neisse to meet with Dr. Franz Nissen, the surgeon who had the clinic built for his busy practice.

Shorter than Georg, Dr. Nissen has lighter brown eyes, a softly bent nose, thick wavy brown hair trimmed closely on the sides and parted near the middle, and a chevron-style mustache tinged with gray. Although 50 years old, he does not need to wear eyeglasses. A crease is deepening between his eyes and up the middle of his forehead. He smiles easily, reflective of his warm personality and optimistic nature. After the onset of WWI, the German command has tasked Dr. Nissen to serve as the surgeon in charge of a 200-bed unit for severely wounded soldiers at the military reserve hospital in Neisse. (In December 1915, the German military would award Dr. Nissen an Iron Cross, II Class, for his services.)

Georg too is a doctor, but of a different kind, a *juris* doctor. Before being called up for German military duty, he was building up a legal practice in Breslau, a city about 55 miles northwest of Neisse. The military has deployed Georg as a field inspector for hospitals for wounded soldiers on the Eastern Front.

The two men meet in Dr. Nissen's office to discuss some legal or administrative matter. They know someone in common: Dr. Speier, a physician practicing in Kattowitz, a Silesian city near the Polish border. Dr. Speier is Georg's brother-in-law and also a *Vereinsbruder* of Dr. Nissen, a member of the same fraternal association.

During the meeting, Dr. Nissen's daughter Edith, who is in Neisse for a visit with her parents, walks in and is introduced. She is 19 and a stunningly beautiful young woman, as photographs attest. She has light-blue eyes, an oval face, a flawless complexion, and light brown hair, fashionably swept up over her head. She has had a privileged upbringing as the surgeon's only daughter. Highly intelligent and self-confident, she works as a teacher in Warmbrunn, sent there to replace a male teacher called up for military duty. She does not accept any pay for teaching, as is the custom for well-to-do young women of that era.

Dr. Nissen introduces his daughter. Georg looks up briefly, says hello, then turns away immediately to continue his discussion with Dr. Nissen. This was unusual for Edith. Strikingly attractive, she was used to having gentlemen fuss and fawn over her, or be flustered when they met her. She was not used to being ignored when an eligible young gentleman met her, so her father's visitor stood out in that respect.

And that's how my grandparents, Georg Fröhlich and Edith Nissen met.

Despite his apparent nonchalance and coolness in the initial meeting, Georg did take notice of Edith. He began courting her. At the time they met, she was teaching and living with her parents' friends, Dr. Sam Freund, a psychiatrist, and his wife, Paula, in Warmbrunn, a town known for its hot springs.

The Freunds' maid at first thought that Dr. Fröhlich must have had significant psychiatric problems because his visits were becoming more frequent. *Er muss aber schwer Nervenkrank sein,* the maid observed. (He must be seriously nervous.) Georg proposed to Edith during a leave from his army service and they became engaged on January 8, 1916. Edith became so excited after the proposal that Dr. Freund gave her a homemade tranquilizer, a sugar cube with *Baldrian Tropfen* (Valerian drops).

Georg had been called to German military duty on August 2, 1914, shortly after the outbreak of war. He showed "exceptional organizational talent" in his role as an inspector and an ability to "overcome administrative obstacles in favor of his hospitals and the wounded," according to an article written many years later about him.[1] "His tireless readiness for action and his striking special amiability earned him special affection and formal recognition by the military authorities, as well as the awarding of the Iron Cross, Second Class in 1917. In the last part of the war, he headed the administration of a large plague hospital in Lodz, Poland."

A picture of Georg in his military uniform shows him as a handsome man in his early thirties. Pinned on his uniform is a ribbon, reflecting his Iron Cross award. He sits on a wicker chair, his dark hair and mustache neatly trimmed, looking very debonair. He wears his pince-nez glasses and high boots. He holds some papers on his lap and a cigarette in his right hand.

After becoming severely ill with dysentery, Georg was released from military service in August 1918, before the end of the war. Edith gathered paperwork for a wartime marriage license and met Georg at a train station in Silesia. They married shortly afterwards.

If photos were taken of their wedding, they did not survive. In a candid shot of Edith and Georg together, taken about a decade later, Edith wears a fashionable, flapper-style, knee length dress and a scarf. She stands in Mary Jane-type strapped shoes with heels. George wears a three-piece dark suit, light shirt, bow tie, a white kerchief folded in his suit pocket and a chain from a watch fob dangling from his vest pocket. He has one hand raised, the other in his pocket. They stand outdoors, looking and smiling at each other. They appear to be engaged in conversation and charmed with each other.

Edith's mother Margarete was not entirely happy with the match. Although Georg was not religious or an observant Jew, Edith's mother worried about his Jewish background, not because of antisemitism but because of her fear of it. Georg's parents, Adolph and Charlotte, were practicing Jews who had both had passed away in the previous century. His grandparents, Hirschel and Marianne Fröhlich, were the first Jewish settlers in Kattowitz (now Katowice).

Margarete's mother, Clara Sophie Borchert née Cohn, was a sister of Ferdinand Cohn, a famous botanist considered one of the founders of the field of bacteriology. Although of Jewish ancestry herself, Margarete Nissen had distanced herself from that heritage. She had had Edith and her two brothers, Rudolf and Ferdinand, baptized and registered as Protestants, and feared that her daughter's marriage would be "a step back into the hole of antisemitism." Margarete's fears were prescient.

After WWI, Georg was appointed as a member of the *Reichsentschädigungskommission* (war reparations commission) in Berlin. He took part in drafting memoranda of the German Reich for the peace negotiations in Versailles, working as an independent consultant on compensation questions in areas such as financial administration, liquidations and personal injury.

Georg returned to Breslau in 1919 to resume his legal practice. In 1920, Georg became a notary, which in Germany is a legal position requiring a law degree plus additional training and qualifications. In 1923, he went back into civil service when he was appointed legal adviser to the Reich Commissioner at the *Reichswirtschaftsgericht* (Reich Economic Court) in Berlin. He then became head of the appeals department for the Reich at the new compensation office in Berlin where he wrote a handbook for internal official use and served as a councillor to the Reich Finance Ministry, again advising on war compensation claims.

In 1924 after the compensation office initiated a ban on promotions, he left civil service to become general counsel to the Engelhardt Brewery Group in Berlin and then returned to legal practice at the Breslau Higher Regional Court. In the later 1920s and early 1930s, he built up a successful law practice, became a board member of Engelhardt Brewery and several stock companies, and served as a legal adviser to the Silesian Mortgage Bank and various industrial companies. He also represented members of the Silesian nobility and large landowners. He retained several junior attorneys to handle the work.

6

CHILDHOOD OF ANDREAS AND SABINE

Most of what I learned about the childhood of my mother, Sabine, came from interviews with her over the years, first during our trip to Mauthausen in 1998 and later during my many trips to visit my parents at their homes in New Jersey between 2000 and 2017. Sabine wrote letters to her Nissen uncles describing her wartime experiences. Many quotes are taken verbatim from those letters, my interviews, her emails and from documents she and her parents had saved. Sabine had a slight foreign accent in English, not the stereotypical heavy German accent. To me, her accent was there but untraceable in origin, probably because she had had to learn so many languages in childhood. Fortunately, many family photographs survived to help visualize the story. These pictures were entrusted to Aryan friends who preserved them for the Fröhlichs when they had to flee Germany, move multiple times in the Netherlands and later go into hiding.

The Births of Andreas and Sabine

Andreas Rudolf Fröhlich was born on October 14, 1921. He arrived during difficult economic times, while Germany was experiencing postwar hyperinflation. We have wonderful sepia pictures of Andreas as an infant and as a young boy with his mother. Edith looks so lovely, radiant and happy in those photos and Andreas, so sweet and shy in front of the camera.

Sabine Gabriele Fröhlich was born at home in Breslau shortly before midnight on January 7, 1927. "My father wanted me to be born on January 8, his engagement day with my mother, and told the doctor so. The doctor told him he could not do anything about it. My mother was relieved." Edith named her daughter Sabine after the heroine of a popular German novel, *Soll und Haben* (Must and Have). The middle name Gabriele was after the daughter of a close friend, the family's pediatrician.

When Andreas was first shown his new sister, he was skeptical the baby was really a girl. *"Aber Sie hat ja eine Bubikopf,"* he protested. (But she has a little boy's head, i.e. short hair like a boy's.)

Edith was a nervous mother, distraught that Sabine was not nursing well enough. She called Dr. Walther Freund, their pediatrician and family friend, who advised her not to worry: *"Fünf Minuten bevor Sie verhungert, wird Sie essen."* (Five minutes before she starves, she will eat.) When Sabine was only a year old, she developed a boil on her head that her grandfather, Dr. Franz Nissen, incised and treated.

Sabine's first 11 years were privileged and idyllic. She had doting parents, a loving and protective older brother, and a housekeeper-nanny who was like a second mother to her. She went to private schools. She had music and dance lessons. Her parents shielded her, for the most part, from the growing ugliness of politics percolating in Germany in the mid-1930s.

Even 70 years after she fled Breslau, Sabine could describe in detail her childhood home, room by room, and its surrounding garden with a gazebo. Her family held onto black & white 5x7 pictures of the interior of that home from the 1930s.

Carmerstrasse 7, Breslau

Sabine's first memories are of the family home on Carmerstrasse 7, a quiet street two blocks from the tram line. "You could see your neighbors. Actually our house and our neighbor's house was one building, just like a twin house. Everything was the same. It was like a duplex. There was Carmerstrasse 7 and Carmerstrasse 9.

"We had a gate that was locked, and if a delivery came, they had to ring the bell, and then somebody had to come to open the door for them, and that was usually Herr Schwartzer, from the couple that lived in the basement.

"I never had a key. I always had to ring the bell when I came home from school and someone always had to be there. My parents were afraid of burglars. I probably could have climbed over the fence at some point, but I don't think I did that. It was pretty high fencing." The fence was a stucco wall, topped with tall decorative ironwork.

On the first floor were the formal dining room, kitchen, her father's study (*Herrenzimmer*) and the *Biedermeierzimmer*, a living room filled with Biedermeier furniture, Persian rugs, paintings, family photographs and a Bechstein grand piano. A wide stairway that split three ways led to the upper floors.

On the stairwell landing to the second floor, opposite a wall of windows, was an antique secretary desk with large drawers that Edith filled with clothes for dress-up play for the children. The second floor held the bedrooms for the Fröhlich family. The third floor had the *Waschküche* (laundry), *Trockenraum* (drying room), and the servants' bedrooms. A woman would come to the house weekly to boil and wash the laundry and hang it up on huge clotheslines strung along the drying room.

Live-in Servants

An elderly couple, the Schwartzers, lived on the ground floor. Mr. Schwartzer maintained the yard, swept the walks, kept the furnace going and opened the gate for visitors. "And when company came, he put on a fancy jacket and opened doors."

Sabine did not think the Schwartzers had any children. "You see, my grandparents weren't nearby, so they were kind of extra grandparents. I could walk in on them. They were very sweet to me. I never bothered them. They always let me stay there and visit with them if I wanted to talk to someone or other in their basement apartment. They didn't seem to have visitors. They were always happy to see me.

"They had a peculiar smell, a smell which was always there. A smell which I really think was a poor people's smell. Not very good body care and so on, but it came with the apartment."[1]

The other family servant was Fräulein Emma who lived on the top floor. Sabine had a close and warm relationship with Emma, regarding her as a second mother. Emma had no children and treated Sabine as if she were her own child. When Sabine had bad dreams at night, she would go to Frau Emma for comfort more than to her mother. When Emma cooked, she allowed her charge to be in the kitchen with her and taste some of the food being prepared, including delicious cake batter.

Mealtimes, Birthdays and Holidays

"I did not have breakfast with my parents," Sabine recalled. "I had breakfast by myself or with my brother. My mother usually stayed in her bedroom, talking on the phone to friends. My father had breakfast at a separate little round table, from that same furniture we still have, with the big backed chairs...

"And we would have breakfast and then march past him on the way to school. I just gave him a kiss. He was happy to see me and happy to see me go. That's when I saw him in the morning. But he ate breakfast alone, and my mother ate breakfast in bed much later. I didn't see her in the morning, really, other than to stop by to say good morning before going to school.

"Sunday dinner was always an occasion. We got a little wine with some seltzer to drink, from age four, five or six. We got the taste of it. And then we had this big joke, running always. Our cook would make a summer fruit soup and, of course, it would be served cold. And we would yell around the house on Sunday morning and say, 'Come quick, the soup is getting cold!' A big, old joke. Dinner was on a very nicely set table with wine glasses for my parents, but we got the seltzer with a little spritz of wine in it, that was our treat.

"After we had the dinner, I would go out and play—or something or another. Dinner was always in the middle of the day, the Sunday dinner was. And the thing was that my father and mother were both there. The other days during the week, I only ate with Andreas, or in the kitchen or with my mother. My father worked, always late, late hours, and if he came home, he worked in his home office, so he was not part of the mealtimes, but on the weekends, he was."

From an email Sabine wrote to granddaughter Laura, May 4, 2000:

My parents had big dinner parties in the house and a special cook would come in for that. She made a lemon cream dessert and I got the bowl to scrape with my finger. The iceman came regularly with a big chunk of ice on his shoulder to put in the icebox. A bowl underneath caught the drips and sometimes overflowed.

At the party, the dinner menu was often venison and I would watch the cook thread thin fat strips through the meat with something like a big needle. Rabbits would come with their skin [on] and had to be hung upside down on the balcony before the skin was pulled off. Chickens and geese had to be plucked; they came with all their feathers and I could help with that.

We had a bakery around the corner and I would be sent to get fresh rolls and usually started eating one on the way home. Another funny thing was going to the butcher and buying 15 Pfennig of raw sauerkraut in a paper bag and eating that on the way home. We had allowances but never bought candy. I think that was not permitted.

Birthday celebrations for children were pretty much like here [US], but we did not have elaborate cakes, usually hot dogs with potato salad and raspberry lemonade.

Birthday for my mother meant a table full of gifts which my father had collected and practical presents from the children. I do not remember anything about my father's birthdays or going to weddings.

Christmas was a big holiday. Gifts were given on Christmas Eve. The room with the tree was off limits for several days and we were summoned by handbell when it was time to go in and look at the presents, with the tree lit up with real wax candles. Everyone had their little table with presents. Of course, sometimes there was a bicycle or other large item sitting next to the table.

My mother got a huge pile of chocolate. We would calculate how long that would last, since she always had some by her bed and would eat chocolate in the middle of the night. It did not affect her teeth; she never needed dentures.

Christmas Eve there would be an elaborate fish dinner, steamed fish and it appeared on the table, head and all, sad. Christmas Day we had a goose dinner. The fat that dripped off the goose was collected during cooking, it congealed and we would eat it on bread, very delicious. Nobody had heard about cholesterol and calories in those days! Well, all this childhood stuff came to an end when I left Germany at age 12 to live in England and your Mom can explain to you why.

Bedroom and Bedtime

Sabine remembered her childhood bedroom as a "big, big" room with a large white or pink bed—she was not sure about the color. Her bedroom had "lots of toys and lots of space and big windows.

"I had a big doll house. I had dolls, but fancy dolls, not something to mother with at all. But I also had other toys. I wasn't completely girlish. It was a big room and it had one door which was a glass door between my room and my brother's room, which was always closed.

And then the other door was the walk-through to my parents' bedroom. It was like two doors with a little space in between.

"My brother's room was his territory. I would go in there to talk to him or he would go to me. I can't remember any toys that he had. He probably did have little metal soldiers and stuff like that. All German boys did, had soldiers. But I know the rooms were adjoining and the door between us was glass and covered with a curtain, a green curtain. We both had very large bedrooms.

"My parents' bedroom had a big attached balcony. They had one bed with two sets of mattresses, *lits jumeaux* (twin beds), built into a platform. If I wanted to see my parents at night, I would go and lie in my father's bed before they went to bed and it was just a short distance for them to carry me back to my bed. I would fall asleep in his bed. I remember that my father would bring me back to my bed after I had been parked there when he went to bed.

"My father was a workaholic. He worked day and night. He sometimes would work all night, smoking and drinking coffee. He had a work room at home, the *Herrenzimmer* (gentlemen's room) which had a built-in settee. I remember going into his room to say good night and the room was blue with smoke. His fingers were yellow from smoking. He had nicotine poisoning twice."

Sabine sometimes left drawings for her father on his bed, and we have a few of those that her father must have saved.

A voracious Reader

"One of my first misdeeds was that I was always reading," she recalled with a smile. "I was a voracious reader and read even when I was supposed to sleep. There were always books in my bed. When somebody came up the stairwell, if they came to the landing, they could see if there was a light on in my room. And the stairwell would creak a little, so whenever I heard a creak, I would very quickly put my flashlight and myself under the blanket so I could read under the blanket because I didn't want to stop reading."

Backyard Memories and Neighborhood Friends

Sabine had fond memories of her large back yard: "We had fruit trees, plum and cherry trees. We had a cherry bush that grew on a retaining wall; it was a climbing cherry. They were really sour cherries, not for eating. But of course, I always ate them as soon as they turned a little bit red, and I got sick.

"I buried a canary in a sardine can under the chestnut tree. A cat got at it...

"We had a lawn, with a circular path around it of little stones, and there was a little pavilion—a gazebo, which we used as a playhouse. The pavilion was covered and that's where I played with my friends."

One of her friends was Eva Kopsik, the daughter of the neighbor's housekeeper and gardener. "We played a lot together because she had no brothers and sisters, so I kind of adopted her as a sister, and we did a lot of playing. And she came over and we played dolls in the pavilion and all kinds of stuff like hide and seek."

Sabine had several neighborhood friends. Ursel Lesser and her sister lived on the corner of her street, and were a few years older than Sabine. Other friends were Liesel Lotte and Marianne Graetzer. Marianne's parents owned a country estate outside of Breslau. Sabine visited them in the country manor where she and Marianne played in haystacks. She remembered big, fancy meals at the estate, with a butler carrying huge platters of food into the dining room.

"Some of the children I went to school with didn't live that close. And, of course, I played on the street. I would ride a bike and my brother's friends were on the street also. And I played soccer with my brother's friends."

She also played hopscotch and table games such as *Mensch ärger dich nicht* (Sorry) and checkers. Winters she went sleigh riding. She remembered sledding down a hill named devil's hill as big time fun. The person who became her best friend was Marianne Küchler who lived nearby. Sabine recalled, "Marianne and I were allowed to cross streets to visit each other. And we could go to stores to buy bread and then to another store and we always got a cookie at each store."

Home Remedies

"For colds and cough you had to drink hot milk with honey, so now I can't stand honey! Cuts got dabbed with peroxide which does not sting as much as iodine. Don't remember warts but when your mother had them, I told her to spit on them and they would go away." *(From Sabine's May 4, 2000 email to Laura.)*

Mother Edith Fröhlich

Sabine saw her mother as a very elegant and stylish woman. Gregarious, congenial and talkative, Edith had a thriving social life. "She was always dressed beautifully. When she went out to parties, the hairdresser came and made her hair wavy. She [the hairdresser] put big tongs into a little Spiritus burner, like a sterno-type flame, and you could smell the heated hair. And she [Edith] would get dressed in front of this big, big mirror and the hairdresser would be there. And then she would go out to some festivity with my father. She was a beautiful woman, and her hair had to be done just right before she went to a party. Sometimes she went alone. When my father just didn't take the time to go, she went anyway. She enjoyed those parties." Women came to the home several times a month to do sewing and make dresses. Edith wore long gowns and beautiful jewelry to some of the parties.

"For dinner parties at home, a special cook, Frau Michaelski, would come in early and cook for the guests. It was an entire day's work to prepare the guests' meals." Sabine was expected to greet the dinner guests before she went to sleep. "I had pink silk pajamas that I had to wear when visitors came to our house. I had to come into the living room, shake hands and curtsey to the guests."

Edith managed the household and worked for some charitable

organizations. "I can't remember the names, but I know she did volunteer for them. She was on the board of some charitable organizations. Caritas, for example, is one of them. It's a Catholic welfare organization."

Father Georg Fröhlich

Georg had a very busy, successful civil law practice. He usually took the tram to his offices on Kaiser Wilhelmstrasse. The tram stop was a short walk from Carmerstrasse. Sometimes he went to work in a private chauffeured car.

Sabine remembered visiting her father's workplace: "It was in a big building with offices. It was on a second floor, and it was very fancy, with very beautiful furniture. It was wide open, with rooms for conferences and stuff like that.

"I remember some of his coworkers, some of the people who worked in his office. And we saw them after the war. The Sonnabends. He was working for my father. And there was somebody else that worked for my father and we [also] met them after the war again.[2] So, he had a legal office with several younger lawyers, handling, you know, the grub work."

The Fröhlich Children's Relationship with their Parents

"My father called me *Leberwurst* because I was always contradicting him. It was a term he dreamed up for me. My father and I had a good relationship. He was tough, but also proud of the fact I was a good scholar, which was a detriment to Andreas. My brother was not that into boyish stuff; he played football, but that's all."

Sabine thought her father was very harsh with her brother for being a poor student. "My mother was protective of Andreas. My father's position was that the son of a doctor [of law] can't fail or repeat a grade. My father was an 'Old Testamentarian.' What's expected of you, you had to produce. Andreas was born in October and put into school in April before he was six years old. He would have benefited from being held back a grade." Andreas had a stutter that subsided as he got older. Though somewhat shy, he still made good friends.

"My father had a temper. He never apologized for his temper. He once stood me up against the wall to slap my face or ear (*Ohrfeigen*). He slapped Andreas too, but also berated him. '*Du faules Luder, du.*' (You lazy lout). It was a terrible thing to say."

Andreas had a close relationship with his mother. Edith was protective of him when Georg was being hard on him for not earning better grades in school. Andreas, in turn, was very protective of his sister who tended not to be very obedient and got into a lot of trouble with her parents. When she cried after being punished, Andreas would come to console her. She remembers that Andreas was always very gentle with her. And he always stuck up for her.

Sabine found it amazing that Andreas never showed any resentment against her for being her father's "pet child," as her mother termed it. "He should have hated me, but he didn't." When Sabine got into trouble, Andreas would take her side and comfort her. "Andreas was a very good older brother, very caring and protective. I think he felt responsible for me.

"When I misbehaved, my mother raised her voice, went to the phone and said she was calling my father in his law office. She would complain to my father: '*Sabine is wider zo ungezogen.*' (Sabine is again so disobedient.) '*Kannst du kommen?*' (Can you come [home]?). I quickly caught on that it was a fake call because of the way she dialed the phone when she made these make-believe calls to my father. It was fake dialing."

Sabine described herself as a terrible tomboy as a child. She preferred wearing her brother's cast-off leather short-pants rather than dresses, and would play soccer with the neighborhood boys while Andreas did the cross-stitch embroidery that she was supposed to do. "He was a good big brother. He did handwork for me because he knew I would get into trouble if it wasn't done."

"The neighborhood boys played soccer on the street and I was allowed to play with them. I wore my brother's *Lederhosen* (leather shorts) to play. My mother was aware of it and didn't approve, but she didn't stop me." Sabine broke her nose during one soccer game, resulting in a nose permanently bent slightly to the left. She wore dresses because her parents insisted on it.

The Birthday Gift Caper

The custom for children in that era was to give hand-made gifts to their elders, such as a drawing or an embroidered cloth napkin, for special occasions. Sabine had no patience for such domestic crafts, preferring to play soccer.

One day, Sabine was waiting at the landing near the bottom of the stairwell for her father to come home from work so she could give him his birthday gift. Her brother, however, was the one who was making the gift, a cross-stitched place mat. She needed to meet her brother first to get the place mat into the gift box before her father arrived.

She saw her brother coming down the stairs to meet her and transfer what she hoped would be the completed gift.

She caught his eye. "Is it finished?" she asked him.

Yes, he nodded back, when just then the front door opened. Her father had arrived home unexpectedly early.

Sabine momentarily panicked. The transfer of the gift into the gift box had not been completed. Her father would discover the subterfuge.

She turned around quickly, bumped into her father and dropped the gift box. "So sorry, Papa," she exclaimed. Her brother understood immediately, rushed down the stairs to gallantly pick up the box for his sister. He dropped the cross-stitch piece as he picked up the box, pretending it had fallen out of the box. Her brother, her knight to the rescue again.

Georg would often joke that Edith had the genders of their children *vertauscht* (criss-crossed).

Vacations

From the email to Laura dated May 4, 2000:

> We would vacation with mother by going to a mountain hotel for several weeks and doing a lot of hiking. My parents went on separate vacations together, since the court vacation did not coincide with school vacations.
>
> My father always would have his secretary accompany them for a few train stops for last-minute dictation. They usually went to Yugoslavia, Menton (France) and Italy, but never with their children. We had a housekeeper-cook, so they could leave freely.

Georg was an avid mountain climber and outdoorsman. He climbed the Grossglockner, the highest mountain in the Austrian Alps. When the Fröhlichs vacationed in the Alps, Edith was always fearful of some mishap during Georg's mountain hikes. He sometimes would be away for days, sleeping in cabins along the hiking trails. He would send postcards with poems he wrote for Edith. She would fret, pacing back and forth at the hotel, waiting for Georg to return from his hike. She could not relax until she saw him walk back into the hotel.

Sabine remembered going on vacations to Austria and Czechoslovakia. Not many pictures of the family vacations exist except for one well documented trip to the seashore town of Zuppot (now Supot, near Gdansk, Poland) on the Baltic Sea. A series of small photos of Andreas and Sabine shows them playing together in the sand in Zuppot and others show them with their parents. Sabine looks to be about one to two years old, Andreas seven or eight. In one photo of the family sitting on the sand, Andreas is leaning over toward his sister, his hand on her shoulder as he whispers into her ear. Another faded photo shows Andreas looking down sweetly to

Sabine while holding her hand. For me, these photos personify sibling affection.

Religion

Sabine believes she might have been baptized as a Protestant because that was her mother's religion at the time of her birth. "I think the Nissens were nominally Protestant, but weren't practicing." Sabine's best guess was that she was somewhere between age three and five when Edith converted to Catholicism and decided to raise her children as Catholics.

"I think I was always Catholic. You know, I made my First Communion in second grade, so I must have started as Catholic. And my mother must have converted before that. Kaete Heidenberger was her best friend and convinced her to become a Catholic. I'd never been to a Protestant church.

"On Sundays, my mother went to a Catholic church, a typical European church building with a tall spire. Sitting still in church was not a questionable item; you knew you had to." Sabine's father did not belong to any religious group until the 1940s when he converted to Catholicism.

School Days

At the age of six, Sabine went to a small private elementary school, the Reinhaut Schüle. It was in an apartment building located just around the corner from Carmerstrasse. "We went up a flight of stairs in an ordinary apartment house to the classrooms. The classes were small." She attended this private school from kindergarten through second grade.

Sabine carried a leather backpack on her walks to school. "I don't remember ever being brought to school. We walked ourselves to school. I may have to walked to school with a bunch of friends, probably with Marianne Küchler. There were sidewalks when we walked to school. We didn't have to cross any streets, in the beginning. I didn't walk with Andreas to school. I think it was just neighborhood kids, maybe. Andreas already went to another school. He was six years older. He didn't go to that school."

While her teachers gave her excellent grades, they also noted in report cards that she should try to talk less in class. Sabine remembers that she was an eager student who had a tendency to raise her hand and shout out answers when teachers directed questions at the entire class.

"I was told I was too talkative, that I was disturbing the class, that I would jump in with my answers." In one report card, her teacher wrote: "*Sabine muss bescheidener wären.*" (Sabine should be more modest.) "That's what they called it. *Bescheiden* means you don't want to be in front of everything. I was jumping in with the answers and didn't give the other kids a chance. That's what I was there. You know, one of those students who always wants to be ahead of the class. That was me."

Music and Dance Lessons

Sabine read music notes before alphabet letters. She began piano lessons at age five before she attended kindergarten. "And I still know some of the pieces I learned," she recalled at age 89. "One is called '*Der Wilde Reiter*' (The Wild Rider) and I could still play it if I had a piano. There were several others that were kind of universal children's pieces on the piano." She later had music lessons for other instruments, including on the "block flute" (wooden recorder), the accordion and lastly, the violin.

"And then my parents decided I should have violin lessons. And there is that one picture somewhere where I look like a violinist [in a top hat and tux with tails]. I don't think I took too kindly to violin. It was too complicated. It was not easy. You have to hold your violin just so, and the bow just so, and in order not to scratch, you have to be very gentle. It wasn't very successful. It was just an idea that I should learn this and have the opportunity, but I didn't take to it. I didn't care for it. Violin lessons were probably just before I left Germany."

Sabine also took dance lessons—ballet and tap. "I learned all the ballet positions in a big room with a bunch of other girls my age and the teacher demonstrating." The dance school was in the vicinity of their house. "I also learned tap and I *loved* it. I loved tap because I could make up my own steps and routines. I would dance for my parents, often to Chopin or Mozart, and then take a big bow in front of them after dancing. I had a pink satiny dress that was just for dancing."

Catholic School and First Holy Communion

For third through fifth grade, Sabine went to a bigger school, a Catholic parish school named Karoleis Borromeus. Sabine skipped a grade in elementary school, but is not sure exactly when. "Probably from second to third. Or from third to fourth. Because I was reading already, and it was because I had nothing to do in school. I was way ahead of everything. I don't know why, but I guess whatever was done at home influenced me. It was just the intellectual influence of my parents."

Sabine had her first Holy Communion at Karoleis Borromeus Church. She and her best friend, Marianne had identical outfits for their first Holy Communion: dresses, shoes and even underwear. "We were like twins. The preparations were very elaborate because we had seamstresses make communion dresses for Marianne and me, matching communion dresses. That was a big part, that we got these beautiful white dresses custom-made, very fancy and smocked, and we got veils. It was a big, church ceremony. I don't think my father came, but my mother came. I don't think my father ever came into the Catholic Church. My brother, I am sure he was there. I do not remember going to his Holy Communion or Confirmation, not at all, because he was six years older.

"The picture of me in a white dress, and a wreath around my head, that was the communion dress. We all had little wreaths on the head. We had white shoes and held a white prayer book." Sabine could not recall having any party or celebration after the ceremony.

Ursuline School

In 1937, Sabine began sixth grade, attending the Ursuline School in downtown Breslau near the Oder River. She commuted there by tram. She had very fond memories of the Ursuline School and its nuns. She loved the teachers at her new school, especially her homeroom teacher, Mater Consolata. "I loved it. I absolutely loved it. I was especially good friends with Mater Consolata. They all had Latin names. She kind of took to me as a child that she could never have. She was very involved with me."

The hated Braids

Sabine particularly hated having her long, dark, fine-stranded hair combed and braided. In pictures, you can almost see her resentment of those hated braids in her hazel eyes as she stares into the camera.

"It hurt and I hated it when my mother or Frau Emma used a comb to unsnarl the knots after my hair was washed." Sabine also disliked the morning ritual of having her hair braided, then having each of the two braids pulled up and pinned with a bow to the sides of her head above her ears. The braiding style was called *Affenschaukeln* (monkey swings), a popular style for German girls in the 1930s.

In 1938, when she was 11, Sabine went to visit her favorite aunt, Tante Rosa (Fröhlich) Speier. Tante Rosa told her she was going to take her for a walk. *"Wir gehen mal nach Frisseur und schnurr die Haare."* (We are going to the hairdresser and having your hair cut.) Sabine remembered feeling a little afraid about the announcement.

"Aunt Rosa probably felt sorry for me after I complained about how much it hurt to have the knots in my hair untangled. The hairdresser didn't know that Rosa wasn't my mother."

The hairdresser cut off the hated braids. Tante Rosa had the braids placed in an empty soap box, tied up with a bow. When Sabine returned home, she presented her parents with the gift box. "They were livid," she recalled.

7

GERMANY, 1930–38

Because she was still a child when she left Germany in 1939, Sabine would not have been fully aware of the precariously changing politics there during the 1930s. Overall, Sabine had many happy memories of her childhood in Breslau. As I undertook more research, it became obvious that my Fröhlich grandparents must have taken great care to shield their children from much of the disturbing political developments during this time, at least until Kristallnacht made normalcy impossible for the family.

I often wondered why the Fröhlich family remained in Breslau so long after Hitler rose to power while their Nissen relatives and other family members and friends began leaving the country. Sabine said her family stayed was because Georg thought the Nazis would be a temporary aberration for Germany. As a WWI veteran and German patriot, Georg initially did not believe that the Nazis would gain power or act on their rabidly antisemitic ideas. And once the Nazis did begin imposing restrictions on those of Jewish ancestry, Georg thought he would outlast the rogues.

Also present might have been an element of defiance, a stubborn refusal to be intimidated or chased out of his own country. And there was the practical consideration: law is not a portable profession. How would he support his family outside of the German legal system? And how could anyone back then fathom a country that would exile and kill its own veterans? Unthinkable.

The impact of Nazi edicts and laws on my grandparents' lives during the 1930s was not a topic I ever discussed with them. I would have to look at other sources to try to reconstruct what it must have been like for them to live through that era.

Although both had Jewish ancestry, Georg and Edith were not part of Breslau's Jewish community. Their children were baptized and attended Catholic schools. Edith, who was registered at birth as a Protestant and later a converted to Catholicism, was active in Christian charitable organizations. Georg was not a member of any synagogue or other Jewish organization. Sabine thought her father was a member of a fraternal organization, likely the Freemasons,[1] based on her mother telling her on some evenings, *"Vati ist in der Loge"* (Father is at the Lodge).

Georg was by all indications an assimilated German. He had served on war reparation commissions, civil service positions formerly closed to Jews. He was a decorated military veteran and had a long history of relatives who had also served in the Prussian and German military. Nevertheless, the Nazi laws of the 1930s were applied to the Fröhlichs and the Nissens because of their Jewish ancestry.

The Nazi racial laws that became known as the Nuremberg Laws did not define someone as a Jew based on religious beliefs but rather on a pseudoscience of race. Anyone who had three or four Jewish grandparents was defined as a Jew, regardless of religious beliefs and practices or whether they self-identified as Jews or not. The Fröhlich family, like many other Germans who had not practiced Judaism for years, became targets of state-sponsored antisemitism and terrorism.

In his memoirs about being a jurist in Silesia, Konrad Wernicke, a cousin of Edith, described the dramatic changes occurring in Germany in the mid-1930s: "With the [Nazi] seizure of power, a racial madness gripped large parts of the population like an epidemic," he wrote. "Incomprehensible and strange were the hate tirades against Jews with whom they [Christian Germans] had lived together for hundreds of years."[2]

Impact on Breslau of Post-WWI Politics and the Nazi Rise to Power

Abraham Ascher's book, *A Community Under Siege, The Jews of Breslau under Nazism*,[3] provides a good deal of background for the Fröhlich family story. Ascher was born in Breslau in 1928—a year after Sabine —and grew up in Breslau. He left Germany at age ten, first for England and later the United States, where he became a history professor. His book focuses on the impact of Nazi propaganda, edicts and actions against Breslau residents deemed Jews under Nazi racial theories.

Breslau is located about 170 miles east of Dresden. A historic city on an ancient trade route along the Oder River, Breslau had grown by 1910 into the seventh largest city in Germany with a population of about 512,000. Roughly 60 percent of its residents were Protestant, 35 percent Roman Catholic and 5 percent Jewish.

Not far from the city, the rich mines of Upper Silesia produced about 40 percent of the country's supply of coal and 25 percent of its zinc. Enterprises within the city turned out machinery, furniture, carpets, musical instruments and leather goods, to name just a few of the most important exports, and over 80 financial institutions powered the economy.

A city of considerable charm, Breslau was known for its fanciful gothic-style town hall, numerous medieval streets, many colorful bridges, attractive monuments and churches, parks, zoo, athletic stadium and rich cultural offerings including theater, opera and orchestra. The city was home to many educational institutions, including the University of Breslau founded in 1702.

After Germany lost WWI, there was a wave of antisemitism blaming Jews for the loss, a pernicious turn of events given how many had

67

contributed to the war effort. In all, some 100,000 Jews, about one-sixth of the total population, had been enlisted in the armed forces, and 78,000 of them served on the battlefront. Twelve thousand Jews lost their lives, 30,000 had received medals for bravery in battle, and 19,000 had been promoted, 2,000 to the rank of officers. Nevertheless, relations between Jews and Christians deteriorated steadily after the war.

The Weimar Republic, Germany's government between 1919 and 1933, was a time of political dysfunction and economic turbulence. The onerous reparation terms imposed on Germany by Treaty of Versailles and postwar hyperinflation compounded the sense of humiliation at losing a war and created a fertile ground for those seeking blame a scapegoat for their national woes.

Although still a clear minority in the city of Breslau, antisemites in the 1920s launched a variety of campaigns to exclude Jews from teaching positions, medical associations and even the boy scouts. The triumph of Nazism in the 1930s, Asher writes, came as a terrible shock to all the Jews of Germany, but the shock may have hit Jews in Breslau especially hard:

> As residents of one of the more liberal cities in Germany, many considered a resurgence of intense hostility, let alone violence, toward Jews inconceivable. For over half a century, from roughly the 1860s to 1933, Breslau Jews had made enormous progress in integrating into German society. A large number had achieved notable success as businessmen, lawyers, physicians, and, to a lesser extent, political leaders; they also played a critical role in maintaining such cultural institutions as the opera, the orchestra, and the theater, and many of their children attended the best public schools.[4]

To the surprise of many, Breslau turned into one of the more ardent centers of Nazi power. In 1932, the city greeted Hitler with substantially larger crowds than Berlin and gave the Nazis a higher percentage of its votes (43.5 percent) than any other large city. In 1933, its leading officials pursued Hitler's policies so avidly that during the first year of Nazi rule even some party leaders in Berlin worried that Breslau was moving too fast in implementing government policies, especially those designed to rid the economy of Jews.[5]

Onslaught of Nazi Decrees in 1933 and Attacks on the Legal Profession in Breslau

Early in the tenure of Edmund Heines, the thuggish *Obengruppenführer* (senior group leader) of the paramilitary Silesian SA or *Sturmabteilung* (storm detachment), Breslau was the scene of the first large-scale attack by Nazis on the country's legal order. On March 11, 1933, about two dozen Nazi SA members in their brown uniform shirts stormed into the Breslau courthouse. They burst into a large conference room where a Jewish lawyer, Ludwig Foerder, was speaking with colleagues. When told to leave, he refused to budge. The Nazis attacked Foerder, grabbing his arm and hitting him on the head with a metal weapon where he had suffered an injury in WWI, causing him to bleed profusely. The Nazis chased other Jewish lawyers and judges out into the street, going room to room screaming for Jews to get out.

A fair number of lawyers, among them many Christians, were appalled by the attack and within hours decided to protest the action by refusing to enter any courthouse. The work stoppage of the lawyers and judges in Breslau lasted a week, but achieved only minor concessions: the SA was ordered to vacate the courthouse and the building was to be guarded by the regular police. Seventeen out of a total of 218 Jewish lawyers were granted special passes that allowed them to appear in court and to continue their legal work. None of the others would be permitted into the building, although they could still practice law.[6]

In mid-March 1933, the government unleashed a press campaign against Jews in the legal and medical professions, claiming that a "Judaization of justice" had taken place in Germany. In fact, there had not been a marked increase since 1919 in the proportion of Jewish judges, although it was true that the proportion of Jews who practiced law was high, about 18 percent of the total in Germany.

Over the next ten weeks or so, the government issued a stream of decrees, excluding Jews from a wide range of institutions. The government ordered hospitals not to grant access to Jewish doctors. Another decree stipulated that all "non Aryans," defined as anyone with one non-Aryan grandparent, were to leave their government civil service positions immediately.

On April 11, 1933, another government decree stipulated that Jews were to be excluded from the law, except for veterans and their relatives. Close to 70 percent of the Jewish lawyers and close to 50 percent of the Jewish judges could still practice their profession, but debilitating restrictions—such as exclusion from national associations of lawyers—were placed on them.[7]

As a WWI veteran, Georg Fröhlich was excluded from some early Nazi decrees. I don't know whether he was one of the 17 out of 218 Breslau lawyers of Jewish ancestry allowed to continue appearing in the Breslau courthouse. Sabine said her father's clients did continue to have him do their legal work, but that he likely had Aryan assistants sign papers submitted to the court.

In a post-WWII, two-page autobiographical summary Georg wrote, "In April 1933, I escaped an assassination attempt by SA men and fled abroad temporarily with my family."[8] And in a postwar job application, he mentioned that he "had a narrow escape with an attempt on my life," but provided no details. I only discovered this information in family papers after my mother's death and long after my grandfather's death.

Sabine never spoke of such an event nor of leaving Germany temporarily in 1933. She was only six years old at the time. The Fröhlich parents obviously did not tell her about the attempted assassination or why they all went abroad. For all Sabine likely knew, it was just another family vacation trip. I have no further specifics about the event, other than the two brief references to it in Georg's postwar writings. I found no information about where or how long the Fröhlichs stayed abroad before returning to Germany.

I wish I could have asked my grandfather about the event and also about how he managed to keep working in the 1930s. His cover letters and applications for positions with the postwar Allied Occupation Forces, however, do give some clues about the impact of those Nazi decrees.

In a cover letter he submitted on July 26, 1945 for a legal position in Allied occupied Germany, he wrote, "Being of Jewish descent (though Catholic by religion just as my wife and daughter are) I lost my employment as a result of Nazi-orders and regulations."

In one application, he listed employment as a *Notar* from 1919 to 1933. A notary in Germany is quite different from a notary public in the United States. In Germany, a notary requires training as an attorney and additional qualifications. German notaries advise clients on legal transactions and draft, authenticate and register legal instruments such as wills, trusts, deeds, corporate registration applications and other such documents. As of 1933, Georg could no longer practice as a notary. He also ceased board membership of several corporations in 1933.

Georg listed his employment from 1911 to 1938 as a *Rechtsanwalt* (lawyer). So he was able to continue practicing as a lawyer in some form or capacity until 1938. His earnings, though, declined steadily in the 1930s. One postwar application asked him to list his annual income from 1931 through 1945. Georg listed 80,000 Reichmarks for 1931 and 1932. In 1933, it dropped to 70,000, and from there a steady decline down to 25,000 in 1938, 15,000 in 1939 and no income at all for six years, 1940 through 1945.

Nazi Decrees abate in 1934 until 1938

From 1934 to 1937, the decrees and violence against Jews abated somewhat. Although their economic circumstances continued to decline, many Jews managed to eke out a reasonably decent living.

Ascher cites a report from the American embassy in Berlin, noting that the authorities in Breslau had published a list of all the Jewish shops shortly before Christmas 1936 to discourage Aryans from patronizing them. Many Breslauers, however, found the publication useful in guiding them where to shop, and "the Jewish merchants did a fine business."[9]

Until the summer of 1937, moreover, 255 Jewish physicians and a smaller number of lawyers remained in practice, the latter in part by resorting to various ruses to conceal their role in legal proceedings. As late as September 1938, Ascher writes, Jews still owned 1,600 enterprises in Breslau itself and another 200 in the suburbs, many of which continued to cater to Gentiles.

The most far-reaching and ominous economic measure was the decrees of April 27, 1938, which ordered all Jews with assets of at least 5,000 Marks to fill out forms listing their possessions in great detail. The decree contained 23 paragraphs of small print that filled two large pages.[10]

On June 25, 1938, the SA in Breslau took several hundred Jews into custody and brought them to a concentration camp, mainly to Buchenwald, where they had to remain about four weeks. Georg was not taken into custody, but likely knew of some who were. The arrests were another foreboding event for what was to occur four and a half months later: Kristallnacht.

8

SABINE'S MEMORIES OF THE RISE OF NAZISM

Sabine heard Adolf Hitler's voice on the radio and on loudspeakers during the mid-1930s. She said that Hitler's voice was "everywhere and inescapable," and that Hitler and his SA Brownshirts became immensely popular in Germany in the 1930s.

Sabine once saw Hitler from a distance at a rally in Breslau in 1935 or 1936. "Yes, he was visiting there [Breslau] and I saw him go by. He always traveled in an open car." Hitler had his arm upraised, doing the *Sieg Heil* (hail to victory) salute. "I remember flags everywhere, the *Hakenkreuz* (swastika) flags, everywhere. Not the German flags, but the Nazi flags."

She remembered hearing Hitler's strident voice—with an Austrian accent—screaming: *EIN VOLK! EIN REICH! EIN FÜHRER!!* It was a refrain she would never forget. She heard Hitler scream slogans, and then the crowds would answer in kind, screaming back the same slogans.

"I knew that Hitler, whom you could hear on every broadcast station, was a very bad man. But I didn't quite differentiate between the Jewish background and Jewish religion, and so on. I didn't quite understand that. But I knew he was our enemy, I knew that he was trying to do us harm. And as I tell everybody, I can still hear his speeches on the radio, this strident voice, and then the masses answering, *EIN VOLK! EIN REICH! EIN FÜHRER!!*"

Sabine remembered the brown shirts worn by the SA. Pro-Hitler rallies were made to look spontaneous, but, in retrospect, she believed they were carefully programmed, with Nazis planted in the crowds. It was easy to incite a crowd with slogans, including *Juden Raus* (Jews out). She heard "*Juden Raus!*" shouted, but did not connect the antisemitic slogans with herself, she said, because she was just a child and a Catholic.

Children were swept up in Hitler's popularity. Many of Andreas' friends joined the *Hitler Jugend* (Hitler Youth Group). Andreas also wanted to join and wear the Hitler Youth uniform. He was very upset when his father would not allow this, nor would he have been accepted into an organization restricted to Aryan children. Andreas joined another group, religious-oriented, which also had a uniform, of which Andreas was very proud. In the picture of him in that uniform, he is smiling with Sabine standing at his side. He poses with a hand on each of her arms and she, with her "monkey swing" braids, smiles too as she leans into him.

Sabine wanted to join the B.D.M. (*Bund Deutscher Mädel*), the female version of the Hitler Youth. She was not as upset as her brother when she could not join because she was less excited about wearing a uniform.

Sabine could not remember exactly how and when she first learned that she had Jewish ancestry. She believes that Andreas' rejection by the Hitler Jugend was her first inkling that she was somehow different from other children. Sabine's Christian schoolmates and neighborhood friends, however, did not ostracize her. They continued to visit and play with her, including her best friend, Marianne Küchler (later Seeger).

Sabine found it incredible that foreign ambassadors living in Germany did not see that Hitler was arming for war. She recalled air raid practices, when sirens went off and everyone would have to seek shelter. She also remembered the required *Verdunklung*, the covering of windows with black curtains so that no lights could be seen outside. The air raid wardens would knock on windows if the house did not look dark enough.

In 1938, at age 11, Sabine had her first asthma attack when her school group had to rush back to Germany from a field trip to Warta, a town near the Czech border. The school group was told to leave Warta because Germany was about to invade and "take back" Sudetenland.[1] That was to be Sabine's last school trip and the beginning of a lifetime of health problems. Hitler had already taken Saarland and Austria with no real resistance. There were rumors of war because the Germans were unsure whether Czechoslovakia would resist the "return" of Sudetenland. Shortly afterwards, Germany took over Sudetenland without resistance.

As the antisemitism and restrictions on Jews increased, some of Sabine's relatives began leaving Germany in the early 1930s. Her uncle, Dr. Rudolf (Rudi) Nissen, was a surgeon and protégé of Dr. Sauerbruch, the foremost cardio-thoracic surgeon of his era and chair of surgery at the prestigious Charité hospital in Berlin. Dr. Nissen was a WWI veteran. He had served as a medic and was wounded in the chest during his military service, causing life-long lung problems.

When the Nazi laws banning Jews from many professional and government positions went into effect in March 1933, the Charité's administrative director called Dr. Nissen and told him to instruct all the non-Aryan physicians under his supervision to submit their resignations as part of a "voluntary elimination." Rudi refused and tendered his own resignation instead. Two months later, he married Ruth Becherer, one of his former medical students, and made plans with her to leave Germany. A US Consul whose child Rudi had treated urged them to obtain US visas, expressing dismay that recent political developments signaled the "outbreak of a barbaric age" in Germany.

The newlyweds visited the Fröhlichs in Breslau and in July 1933 went to Paris, intending to take a train to the coast, travel onto England and then board a ship in Southampton for the USA. Shortly before their scheduled train departure, Rudi received a telegram from his mother in Neisse asking him to contact a Philipp Schwartz in Zurich. Schwartz had been retained by the Turks to reach out to sacked German professors for possible appointments at Turkish universities. The Nissens postponed their boat trip. Rudi was invited to head a surgical clinic and offered a professorship at Istanbul University. He accepted and he and Ruth emigrated to Turkey, arriving there on August 1, 1933.[2]

Sabine's other Nissen uncle, Ferdinand (Ferdi) Nissen, Ph.D., was an economics professor at the University of Frankfurt. His wife, Margarete (Gretel) was an Aryan, beautiful, stately and blue eyed. Ferdi was fired from his position in 1933 because of the Nazi laws. He left Germany with his wife and daughter Beate, first for Switzerland and then later joined his brother in Turkey, where living conditions proved quite difficult for his family.

Members of the Fröhlich family left for England, South America and other destinations. Friends of Georg and Edith began evacuating their families. Their friend Dr. Freund, a client of Georg and Sabine's pediatrician, sent his two children to boarding schools in Switzerland in 1936.

Edith's mother Margarete never fully recovered from the premature death of her husband Franz in 1928. Franz Nissen developed a severe bacterial infection after cutting his hand during emergency surgery on a child and he died within days of sepsis. Margarete Nissen was bereft as a widow. After Nazi laws forced her two sons to leave Germany, she committed suicide in 1937.

Georg, however, stayed on in Germany. While well aware of the Nazis' ascension to power, propensity for violence and enactment of stream of antisemitic measures, Georg thought the enthusiasm for Hitler would be just a temporary aberration. He considered Hitler an extremist nut and believed the sensible majority of

Germans would prevail and vote Hitler and his Brownshirts out of power.

Then too, the German government sent mixed messages. In 1932, Georg received a certificate signed by President von Hindenburg thanking Georg "for his faithful services" on the reparations commission. The Reich sent Georg a certificate in 1935 honoring his military service and award of a military cross in WWI. The certificate, issued "*Im Namen des Führers und Reichskanzlers*" (In the name of the Führer and the Reich Chancellor) and stamped with the German imperial eagle and the Nazi swastika, was signed by the police chief in Breslau. Perhaps it lulled Georg into believing that he as a veteran would remain exempted from the most onerous Nazi decrees and actions.

Memories of the Fröhlichs in the 1930s

In his memoir, *From Munich to Washington D.C.*, Peter Heidenberger, a friend of Andreas, recounts:

Some of my parents' Jewish friends emigrated before the borders closed. The Fröhlich family was among those. Dr. Georg Fröhlich was a respected lawyer in Breslau. My parents knew the family well when we lived there in 1932, before the Nazis came to power. As a 10-year-old, I attended more than one slumber party at their house as a guest of their son Andreas. Little did I know that at the age of 19 he would be killed in Mauthausen.

Andreas was not the athletic type, but a rather studious boy. At night we rehashed conversations we had heard at the dinner table. I remember clearly Dr. Fröhlich had said, "The plate faces can never win the next election." (*Die Tellergesichter können niemals die nächste Wahl gewinnen*). I had never heard the expression "plate faces" before. Dr. Fröhlich was referring to the round hats worn by the storm troopers as they demonstrated for the 1932 parliamentary election. We boys had the impression that each of our parents was confident these dumb radicals could not win many votes. Despite these predictions, the Nazis did end up the strongest party, even though they did not obtain a majority.

Hoping that the Nazi nightmare would blow over, the Fröhlich family stayed in Breslau until 1939.[3]

Sabine's cousin, Beate Nissen, daughter of her uncle Ferdinand and aunt Gretel Nissen, remembered visiting the Fröhlichs in Breslau in 1936. Because Beate's mother was Aryan, she and her mother were able to travel safely from Turkey, where they had temporarily emigrated, back to Germany to visit relatives and friends. Gretel had lost 20 pounds because of her revulsion of the poor sanitary conditions in Turkey. Gretel hoped to recuperate in Germany, for skinny Beate to gain some weight and to access funds the family had left in the country.[4]

Beate described Andreas as tall and slim with dark hair. During her visit with the Fröhlichs, Andreas invited Beate to go upstairs with him to see his ham radio. She recalled her delight that he allowed her to use his ear phones to listen in. "He was very nice, a sweet boy."

In 1937, Rudi Nissen became increasingly concerned about Turkish economic and military ties with Nazi Germany, and even more so with the deepening prospect of a war in Europe that might engulf Turkey. (Turkey would remain neutral in WWII.) He resolved to relocate to the United States. Rudi and Ruth Nissen left Renate, their three-year-old daughter, with Edith in Breslau while they made a month-long trip to the United States to explore opportunities there. Upon their return to retrieve their daughter, Rudi received a telegram to come to Budapest for an urgent operation on an important person before returning to Turkey. Rudi called the Turkish ministry about the request and asked that his nurse assistant and surgical instruments be sent to Budapest. Sabine remembered being in her living room (*Biedermeierzimmer*) when her Uncle Rudi received a call from Turkey.

Both uncles Rudi and Ferdi would obtain visas and emigrate with their families to the United States by 1939. Ferdi was able to find a job in 1938 in Boston as the assistant to the president of Gilchrist's department store. The Jewish owners of the store had pledged to help a few immigrants by giving them jobs. Rudi had been offered a position as a surgery research fellow at Massachusetts General Hospital. Rudi, Ruth—now pregnant with their second child—and Renate arrived in the US in July 1939, just two months before the outbreak of war.

9

KRISTALLNACHT, THE NIGHT OF BROKEN GLASS

Kristallnacht, the night of November 9–10, was a watershed event for Germany and Sabine's family. From Sabine's perspective, Kristallnacht happened without warning, but in retrospect she understood that it must have been orchestrated.

Isolated outbreaks of violence against Jews had occurred before Kristallnacht. Kristallnacht, however, unleashed mass-scale violence against Jews and massive destruction of property owned by Jews throughout Germany. The pretext for a night of cataclysmic violence against Jews nationwide was the assassination of a German diplomat, Ernst vom Rath, by a 17-year-old German-born Jewish boy living in Paris.

Georg Fröhlich's law office was on the first story, one flight above the ground floor, so his office was not destroyed during Kristallnacht, but his sense of security was shattered. "My father went temporarily to another house. And that's when my father finally believed the Nazis were here to stay." The Fröhlichs' life as a German upper-middle class family in Breslau would unravel rapidly.

Sabine was 11 when Kristallnacht happened, still too young to comprehend the full significance of that event for herself and her family. "I went to school on a tram after Kristallnacht. I saw the wrecked stores and burning buildings... I saw all these looted stores on my way to school."

That afternoon, the Ursuline nuns would not let Sabine go home because they did not know what would happen next and were afraid for her. "The nuns organized with my mother that I should stay there overnight. They had plenty of room because they used to have a boarding school, so there was a whole empty dormitory." Fräulein Emma, the family housekeeper, brought some nightclothes for Sabine to the school.

Sabine does not know how the nuns knew her parents had Jewish ancestry, but thinks that Edith must have called the nuns and informed them. Sabine spent two or three nights in the former boarding school section of the school, next to the convent. Her mother brought her clean clothes.

"It was kind of goofy because there was this whole dormitory. I was right next to the convent where the nuns slept, which was, of course, locked. So I was all alone in a big room with a lot of beds.

"It was pretty lonely. But I just think I was 11 years old, and it was a little adventure and it was different. It didn't sink in that this was something, the harbinger of things to come. No, it just happened. When you are 11 years old, you don't really look into the future and connect what happens now with something that might happen in the future. You just go day by day. Just what's happening today."

Sabine ate meals with the nuns. "They set up a little table for me separately, but I ate in their dining room." The nuns did not discuss with her why she was being kept at school. "Nobody had to say anything; they just did it. They're not letting this little girl go home because she's in danger... They just kept me." After several nights, Sabine went home.

On November 15, 1938, the Nazis issued an edict expelling all Jewish children from public schools. Because Sabine attended a Catholic school, I originally thought that this edict had not applied to her. She had told me, "Yes, I continued to go to school there [Ursuline School] until plans were all ready that I could go to England. That was later."

But I learned that my supposition and Sabine's memory were not accurate. My brother found a statement written postwar by Maria Consulata Gevieuer (Sabine's favorite nun) that Sabine had indeed been expelled from the Ursuline School in late 1938:

> Sabine Fröhlich, born January 7, 1927, formerly living in Breslau (Germany) 7 Carmerstrasse was my pupil in the third and fourth form of the Secondary School of the Ursulines in Breslau in 1937/38 until the Half-Arians and Non-Arians [sic] were expelled by the Nazi-Government. Sabine was the youngest pupil in her class, but owing to her talents and her diligence, she was one of the best. Even more than that weighs her good character, her kind and cheerful heart. She was a good comrade to the other pupils; even after the expulsion she exchanged friendly letters with them.

> After having been obliged to leave our school she still had private lessons in Catholic Religion with me as long as she stayed in Breslau...

We have letters, drawings and photos that Sabine's Ursuline classmates and teachers sent her in March of 1939.

Sabine was only 11 when she was expelled. It happened during the tumultuous time for her family after Kristallnacht. Sabine did not remember the expulsion from the Ursuline School. Perhaps she blocked out this event. But I strongly suspect her parents protected her from this blow. How would you—could you—explain to an 11-year-old, a stellar student, the irrational, unconscionable grounds for why she was being barred from her school and the company of her classmates and teachers? Easier and kinder to shield her and tell her that plans are almost ready to send her to school in England.

The Aftermath of Kristallnacht in Breslau

SS-Oberführer Fritz Katzmann gave a preliminary report of the results of Kristallnacht in Breslau to his superiors on November 10, 1938. The property toll included:

- 1 synagogue burned
- 2 synagogues demolished
- 2 Jewish social halls demolished
- 1 building of the Society of Friends demolished
- at least 500 Jewish shops completely demolished
- about 10 Jewish inns demolished
- about another 35 Jewish businesses destroyed

The Gestapo rounded up 2,471 men (somewhere between a fifth and a sixth of the total Jewish population of the city) and sent them to Buchenwald. The events in Breslau were part of a national pattern. That night, Nazis arrested about 30,000 males between the ages of 18 and 80 and sent them to one of three concentration camps, Dachau, Buchenwald or Sachsenhausen. More than 100 people died; 400 synagogues were destroyed. Nazi officials initiated the attacks, in most cities by the SA division, but in Breslau by the SS.[1]

Of all the horrors visited upon the Breslau Jews before and during Kristallnacht—economic deprivation, the destruction of synagogues, interruption of education, endless humiliations in the streets— none was as terrifying as the disappearance of over 2,400 men during the pogrom. No one knew where they had been taken or what their fate would be. Relatives made desperate attempts to obtain information about the whereabouts and circumstances of their loved ones, but at first had little success.[2]

Asher's book describes atrocious conditions and mistreatment in the camps. Before being released, inmates had to sign statements that they had not been mistreated or observed mistreatment. A former judge in Breslau committed suicide the first night by using his hidden pocketknife. Prisoners in the overcrowded, unsanitary barracks became ill and died. Fortunately, Georg escaped arrest and internment on Kristallnacht.

Georg's brother Eugen, however, was not as fortunate. Eugen, who owned a large drug store in Munich, was arrested on Kristallnacht and sent to Dachau concentration camp for several weeks. He was released after being threatened and forced to sign over his assets to a trustee appointed by the Nazis. The proceeds from these assets were to be used to pay a tax of 140,000 Reichmarks for the privilege of fleeing Germany. Eugen had already applied for visas to Britain for his family. Eugen, his wife Ella and their two children would leave for England in early 1939.

10

NAZI EDICTS AFTER KRISTALLNACHT: THE VISE TIGHTENS

The Fröhlich parents remained in Breslau for nearly eight months after Kristallnacht, enduring increasingly oppressive measures imposed by the Nazis while they planned the family's evacuation from Germany.

First, the local Nazis demanded 180,000 Marks from the Jewish community in Breslau to cover the cost of cleaning up the debris from the attacks on November 9–10. On November 12, the government announced that an "atonement penalty" of one billion Marks would be levied on the Jews, thereby explicitly blaming Jews as a group for both the assassination of Rath and the destruction that followed.

An Ordinance of Implementation, issued on November 21, spelled out the procedure for collecting the penalty. Jews with assets at more than 5,000 Marks were to surrender 20 percent of their wealth, the precise amount to be determined by officials after reexamination of the declarations submitted to the authorities in compliance with the ordinance of April 27, 1938. The payments were due in four installments.

On December 14, 1938, prime minister and general field marshal Hermann Göring sent a 13½-page memorandum regarding "the Jewish question." A central point of the memorandum was that the government attached the greatest importance to the seizure of Jewish assets then underway. The seizure, Göring stated, "affects most powerfully the general economic interests of the country," and he also made clear that the program of "dejudaization both of business enterprises and of Jewish properties and other valuable possessions may be implemented by force."[1]

And next comes the passage in Ascher's book about my grandfather protesting the Nazi tactics used in the "aryanization" of his property:

> Occasionally, Jews threatened with aryanization of their property protested the strong-arm methods used against them. Late in 1938, the attorney Georg Fröhlich informed the commissioner of Aryanization that he had already made arrangements to hand over to the "Aryans" three properties that belonged to him and his wife, and he could therefore not understand why several "gentlemen" from the *Deutsche Arbeitsfront* (Labor Front—the Nazi organization of trade unions) had badgered his wife, during his absence, for "urgent explanations" and had forced her to appear at their office.

> In a tone of defiance, Fröhlich declared that "if I do not receive information to the contrary I believe that I would be justified in assuming that I can proceed with the aryanization of the properties in the manner already initiated by me without the cooperation of the gentlemen from the Arbeitsfront." Fröhlich ended with a request for a quick decision on the arrangements he had made. The archive does not contain a reply from the commissioner, but we can assume that he did not take kindly to Fröhlich's letter.[2]

When I was growing up, I was told the reason the Fröhlich family had to leave Germany and go into hiding in Holland was because "Opa Fröhlich had spoken out against the Nazis." Ascher's passage shows there was some truth to that explanation. I believed that story until I was 20-years-old when an elderly aunt inadvertently revealed the primary reason for the family's peril: their Jewish ancestry.

Sabine told me that her father had entrusted some of his properties to an Aryan colleague who instead of holding them, had sold or absconded with them.

The pace of emigration from Breslau, as from other regions of Germany, had increased throughout 1938, but after Kristallnacht the pace accelerated rapidly. The Nazis encouraged Jews to leave Germany while simultaneously enacting and enforcing decrees to make their departure more difficult. Those who were lucky enough to obtain visas had to surmount other hurdles because the Nazis placed numerous restrictions on the assets and personal belongings that emigrants could take abroad to help build a new life. Jews were forced to make difficult decisions and to plead with the authorities for permission to ship items that would enable them to make a start in their new home.

Once they emigrated, they faced other anxieties: learning a new language, finding employment, locating good schools for their children, and adjusting to local climate and customs. They constantly worried about the family and friends they had left behind, and they tried hard to fill a deep void, the absence of a circle of loved ones.[3]

In addition to measures to impoverish them, a central feature of the Nazi campaign against Jews after Kristallnacht was a series of decrees designed simply to isolate and humiliate their victims. In November 1938, the authorities prohibited Jews from attending performances in theaters, movie houses or concert halls open to Gentiles. Jews were also not to be admitted to museums, public libraries, zoos, swimming or sports facilities, or parks.

Public benches in Breslau carried signs "Für Juden verboten" (Forbidden for Jews). The signs, posted in the middle of the upright part of the benches, were so small, 5 centimeters by 35 centimeters, that older people or nearsighted people often did not see them and would sit down. If the police spotted them, they immediately took them away.

Jews also were not allowed to walk together in groups of more than two. Nor were they allowed to remain standing on street corners. Jews with "non-Jewish" first names were required to adopt the middle name of "Israel" or "Sara."[4]

Kristallnacht and the anti-Jewish measures in the following months removed any doubt about the viability of a future in Nazi Germany—even for a patriot and war veteran such as Georg.

Cousin Beate remembers visiting the Fröhlichs after Kristallnacht

In an interview in June 2015, my mother's cousin, Beate, recalled her last visit to the Fröhlichs in Breslau in 1938, shortly after Kristallnacht. Beate and her mother, Gretel Nissen, were on their way from Turkey to the United States to join Beate's father, Ferdi. They had booked passage on a boat from Germany:

> I remember that Edith took me to the dentist. And I remember she ran the bath water for me. And I remember she had maids. I remember picking her [Sabine] up at school with her mother, I guess. She had on a Loden Mantel, sort of khaki-colored coat, not very attractive. We were there at the Fröhlichs' house for several days. And I remember them shuddering when the bell rang and Georg going to hide. So he knew we were in danger. This was in 1938, the visit before we left for New York. I think I made an error in my biography. I wrote it was 1939 but it was 1938.

Sabine explained that a Loden Mantel was a dark green, almost military-like coat, very warm and practical for winter months. Mater Consolata continued to tutor Sabine privately after the Nazi edict evicting all Jewish children from non-Jewish schools; it was probably from one of these private lessons that Beate remembers collecting Sabine.

Even though Beate's father had left Germany five years before Kristallnacht, he was still expected to pay atonement taxes. In my grandfather's files, I found a letter, dated April 17, 1940, from the *Finanzamt* (tax office) in Berlin to Dr. Ferdinand Nissen relating to the *Judenvermögensabgabe* (Jewish property tax). Ferdi apparently had requested a waiver or reduction of the tax on property he still must have owned in Germany. Georg might have assisted Ferdi with this request.

The tax office response was curt:

> Jewish property tax can only be waived in very special exceptional cases. A strict standard must be applied during the examination. The levy is an atonement.

> You do not have a very special exceptional case. I therefore reject the waiver or a reduction of the further partial amount of the fee. A new determination of the taxable assets does not take place.

The short missive is stamped with the German imperial eagle atop the Nazi swastika. Being stripped of his job and academic career seven years earlier and being forced into exile were insufficient grounds to be relieved of the atonement levy.

By the time WWII broke out in September 1939 somewhat over half of Breslau's Jewish population had left.

11

SABINE AND ANDREAS EVACUATED TO ENGLAND

Kristallnacht finally burst Georg's blind patriotism and optimism that the Nazis were just a passing phenomenon. Sabine termed it her father's wake-up call. Sabine believed that after Kristallnacht, her father and brother left Breslau for a few days to stay with the Heinemans, family friends in Aachen, a town on the German border with the Netherlands. When Georg returned to Breslau after several days, he and Edith began planning their family's flight from Germany.

The Fröhlich parents first sought to safeguard their two children while they dismantled their home and business, and liquidated what assets they could. The hope was to obtain visas to join relatives in the United States. Edith's two brothers, Rudi and Ferdi Nissen who had emigrated to the US, would vouch for the Fröhlichs.

Andreas Evacuated First

Andreas was the first to be evacuated. He stayed in Aachen with the Heinemans, whom the Fröhlichs had met and befriended during vacations in Menton on the French Riviera. Mr. Heineman owned a factory in Aachen. Andreas was with the Heinemans at Christmas 1938.

In a letter dated December 17, 1949, the Heinemans' son, Hendrik, wrote to Sabine about his memories of Andreas and that Christmas: "Eleven years ago we celebrated Christmas with Andreas, that was before he went to the monastery to Pater Adams, I remember still everything as if it were today. Andreas made long poems for us and was very happy that day. How often I think of those times..."

The plan was to have Andreas stay in Aachen, and from there, for him to cross the Dutch border to stay with Camillian monks at a monastery in Vaals, a town in the province of Limburg in the Netherlands. The monks, headed by an abbot named Pater (Father) Adams, ran a Catholic boys' school and a farm at the monastery.

Then suddenly the plans were disrupted, and Andreas returned home to Breslau. Decades later, Sabine wrote to a daughter of the Heinemans to ask why. In an email dated March 28, 2014, Ursula Rickenberg (formerly Heineman) answered:

> Why did my parents send Andreas back to Breslau? Just after Kristallnacht, my brother, Karl, a few months younger than Andreas, had to leave Berlin where he was attending an international school while living with a rabbi's family. The rabbi had been dragged away, and Karl had to leave. So he was sent by my parents to a Jewish camp for boys in Holland. My father was arrested and spent a brief time in jail in Aachen but he was released because my mother pleaded with the Police that he would die as he was thought to be a severe diabetic. He was released, but his brother Otto was sent to a concentration camp. At that point Otto's oldest boy, Herbert, was sent with Karl to Holland. Andreas was not safe and probably your parents instructed him to be sent home.[1]

In a second attempt to cross the border, Andreas was able to make it from Breslau to the monastery in Vaals, Holland. Sabine recalled, "Pater Adams was head of the Camillians. They were a Catholic order. Andreas was taken over the border in Aachen and taken in by the Camillians because the Heinemans had a connection with Pater Adams. And they kind of pushed him over the border somehow. Vaals is in Holland, it's a border town. If you are in Vaals, you can stand with two feet in two countries."

Pater Adams was able to find a Catholic pre-seminary school for Andreas to attend in England. Andreas traveled first by train from Vaals to Amsterdam and then on to Brussels. From there, Andreas went to a port and took a boat to England to enter the pre-seminary school, St. Edmund's College. The school is on a spacious and beautiful campus on a hill overlooking the town of Ware, about an hour's drive north of London.

Andreas kept a diary. The longest entry in the diary is dated Easter, 1939. Andreas, a deeply religious young man, wrote the entry when he was in Brussels on his way to England. Translated from German, it reads:

After many difficulties and searching, partially with success, partially with no success, and planning, I, Andreas Fröhlich, run out of family and home, am in Brussels. Fate has been hard on us, but courage and trusting in God have been the only factors which could help.

Of course, I am very grateful, that in the middle of great need, I have found people who are helping me with my problems. Especially I want to mention Pater Adams, and the fathers and sisters of the Camillian monastery in Vaals, and my relatives in Amsterdam. I could tell them and thank them for their assistance. God will reward them.

Since I was forced by law to leave school all of a sudden, I came to the big question of choosing a profession. Only two areas would be possible for me. Either philosophy or theology. Of these two areas, I choose, after a long process of weighing/consideration, theology. I also wanted to thank my uncle for all the good care to help me fulfill my wish. I am well aware of the great sacrifices which I will have to make and know that any practical profession must be considered if it will be a blessing to help my parents. This is the point which I had to look at especially, most beautiful and highest would be if I could study in the Vatican and bring

God's holy gospel to the world. "Go and teach the word of God to all people."

There are not many entries in the diary. Pages were ripped out. Sabine believed that her mother removed passages she considered too dangerous to keep in case the diary was confiscated during their years in hiding.

Preparations to evacuate Sabine via the Kindertransport

To prepare to evacuate Sabine from Germany, Edith and Georg gathered Sabine's health and school records. The Ursuline School provided an *Übergangszeugnis* (transfer certificate) for Sabine Fröhlich, listing her grade level and her performance in a wide range of subjects, indicative of a rigorous classic Catholic school curriculum. The ratings were: *"gut"* (good) for religion, German, English, French, history, geography, mathematics and needlework; *"befriedinggut"* (satisfactory) for drawing, art and handwriting; *"sehr gut"* (very good) for music and singing, and finally, for biology, a somewhat illegible notation, possibly the word for exceptional.

The dates on the school certificate are of note. Sabine's last day of attendance at the Ursuline School is listed as November 17, 1938, exactly two days after the Nazi edict expelling all Jewish students from non-Jewish schools. The date of the certificate itself is November 28, showing the Fröhlich parents were moving quickly to gather the necessary paperwork to safeguard Sabine.

In addition to signing the school transfer certificate, Mater Consolata provided the equivalent of a short letter of reference stating:

Sabine Fröhlich in line with her good talent, was lively and diligent in class. She is polite and open toward teachers and actively participated in community life. Through her unassuming and helpful nature, she has always been a good companion to her classmates.

Three weeks later, on December 20, 1938, a Dr. K. Klinke signed a health certificate for "Bela Sabine Froehlich" stating that he had examined her in detail and that she was "completely healthy, physically and mentally, and free from infectious diseases, in particular tuberculosis and trachoma."

The Fröhlichs obtained a passport for Sabine, issued on January 3, 1939. The passport, *Reisepass, Nr. 5139*, lists her name as Bela Froehlich. The German Reich assigned her a Nazi-sanctioned Jewish name in lieu of what it deemed the non-Jewish name of Sabine. The Nazis had taken away her education and now, her name. A large "J" for Jew was stamped on the front of her passport alongside a depiction of an eagle perched on top of the Nazi swastika.

Lastly, the Fröhlichs received a certificate, dated January 11, 1939, from Kinnaird Park School in Bromley, England stating: "We have given a free place in our school to Sabine Froehlich for a period of at least two to three years or until she should emigrate overseas."

So by mid-January 1939, just after Sabine turned 12, and two months after Kristallnacht, the paperwork was ready to evacuate their daughter, as were the transportation arrangements. Sabine received new clothes and a suitcase for the trip to England.

Many years later, Sabine's friend Marianne Küchler told her how intensely jealous she was of her because of that little suitcase. It was made out of pigskin leather and had a pinkish tone.[2] In a photograph taken the day of her departure, Sabine is standing on the sidewalk in front of her home on Carmerstrasse, holding her little suitcase. She is wearing a warm coat, white knit hat and poses with her mother, Frau Schwartzer and Fraulein Emma. She is smiling at the photographer. She will never return there.

Sabine does not remember exactly what she was told about leaving home or why. "We knew a lot of people who were leaving. So I knew a lot of our friends are leaving. And for me it was kind of a lark. I was getting this new outfit of clothes. I got this little leather suitcase. And I was going to go on a train. And I was going to go on a boat. It was an adventure. I had no idea that, in effect, my parents are giving me up to save me, that I didn't know." That thought did not occur to her until years later. "After the war, more or less, when we were together and I realized what they had done. They had sent me off, you know, to save me. And luckily they survived too."

Sabine was one of about 10,000 children in the Kindertransport, children evacuated from Germany and placed with families in Britain before the war. In reaction to Kristallnacht, newer German immigrants in England had organized the Kindertransport and located families and schools to take in the child refugees.

Sabine's chaperone for this journey was Ursel Lesser, another girl of Jewish origin, aged 14 or 15, who lived on the same street as Sabine. The two girls took a night boat from Bremerhaven to England. Ursel's younger sister, about 13, went to England on a separate transport, as did her friend Marianne Graetzer. Two other Breslau children sent to England as part of the Kindertransport, and with whom Sabine kept in touch, were Claire and Ulla Freund, daughters of friends of the Nissens.

Mrs. Giles, a German emigrant and teacher at Kinnaird Park School, was the one who had facilitated bringing in German refugee children, giving them places at the school and organizing homes where they could stay while in England.

"She got quite a few into that school and another school. There were hardworking people who were trying to find a better place for us. Pretty amazing. Pretty amazing," Sabine commented in an interview in 2016. "Everything was on blind trust, you know. Now you would be suspicious if someone wanted to do this, maybe for money, but at that time it was, 'We do this for you and it's proper to do it.' It's a very different atmosphere now where everyone becomes suspicious."

Stay in England

In England, Sabine was sent to live with an American family, the Smiths, from St. Louis, Missouri. She described Mr. Arnold Smith as a jolly fellow, with a twinkle in his eye. Mr. Smith worked for

Monsanto. "I remember Mr. Smith being a tall man with a mustache and a booming voice, very, very friendly."

Mrs. Arnold was warm and motherly, with "a big bosom where I could cry. And they really did everything to make me feel at home and comfortable and even tried to learn a few German words and so on and so on. It was a welcome into a family that really wanted to do this.

"I was brought to this big house, with a couple who had four daughters, but one of them didn't live at home. I think she was somewhat retarded. And I was kind of like in the middle age group with them. Sandy was older, Denny was younger and Esther was the youngest."

Although Sabine had learned English in school in Germany, she initially had difficulty understanding the American English spoken by the Arnold family. "I had had some English. The only difference is that the Smiths were Americans and they spoke a very nasal English and it took me a while to understand them."

The Smiths lived in a big Tudor-style house with beautiful furniture. Outdoors they had a big yard and a formal English garden tended to by a gardener. The Smiths also had a cook. Sabine remembers the food there as being very good.

Initially she was very homesick. "I did cry, and then I would go to Mrs. Smith and sit on her lap and get it over with that way. She never said anything [about the home sickness]; she just said, 'Come here' to sit on her lap."

The teachers at Kinnaird Park School[3] were welcoming and pleasant. The teachers made her change her handwriting style from the German script to printed letters, a source of some difficulty, but she liked the school, learned to play tennis, and earned good grades, while at times becoming very homesick.

Kinnaird Park was not Catholic, nor were the Smiths. "It was '39, I just turned 12. I was put into a classroom that I could fit in and assigned to sports that I could learn." She was not sure of the grade level she was placed in, believing it may have been in the "Fourth form [class] or something like that. That's what they call it. I was older than the children in my class because I still had to learn my English."

Nevertheless, Sabine felt that she adapted well to the new school despite the different language. "I rather quickly learned the proper English. Of course, they also tried to change my handwriting. Every country does that. So I had a little trouble with that. The teachers were all very nice and Marianne Graetzer and I were in the same class. But there were others, and also in other schools, you know, and Ulla Freund and her sister Claire were also with an English family in another school."

Kinnaird Park was big into sports, Sabine said. "I had a choice of doing field hockey or tennis, and I preferred tennis, so that's where my tennis comes from. Because it [sports] was a subject, every day there was gym, so it was part of the curriculum. And it wasn't too difficult to follow the instructions."

Sabine enjoyed living with the Smiths. "I was just part of the family, in the middle age range between the girls. So, we goofed around a lot. I remember doing handstands against the big wall in the bathroom after showering. We had showers together and then we just did headstands for exercises. I was one of the ones who could stand up the longest... I shared a bedroom with Denny, I think. I interacted with the girls a lot, except, of course, Esther was the little kid whom we teased a lot."

Sabine also remembered going on outings with the Smiths in their big American car. "Yes, we went for rides in a car. We went to the seashore at some point, and things like that, so there was always something going on. I don't remember ever being bored. There was a big yard, big garden. And it was a time where I really felt comfortable and I wasn't worried about my parents because I really didn't know what to worry about."

She had no memory of visiting her brother at St. Edmund's College during her stay in England, even though she feels that the Smiths must have taken her there at some point.

According to a letter dated May 29, 1939 from the headmaster of St. Edmund's to Georg Froehlich (substituting an "e" for the German umlaut is common in English), the Smiths did indeed take Sabine to visit her brother.[4] The headmaster wrote:

> *Dear Dr. Froehlich,*
>
> *As far as we can judge, your son shows no signs of having been spoiled by anybody; up to date, he shows every sign of being a very well-behaved and industrious young man. It is of course impossible yet to say how much progress he will make with his studies, but we will hope for the best.*
>
> *Yesterday a Mr. and Mrs. Smith called down to see him, and took him out to tea. I believe they brought his sister down as well. Fr. McKenzie, the Housemaster of Douglass, has immediate charge of the boy, and he saw Mr. and Mrs. Smith when they came, and allowed Andreas to go out with them.*
>
> *I have already had a satisfactory letter about financial matters from Mr. Reid.*
>
> *With kind regards,*
>
> *Yours sincerely,*
>
> *(signature) Thomas Sherlock*
>
> *Headmaster*

The letter was addressed to Carmerstrasse 7, Breslau, Germany, so it shows the Fröhlich parents were still in Germany in late May 1939. The letter also demonstrates Georg's ongoing concern and harsh judgment that Andreas was spoiled and not studious.

12

MOVE TO THE NETHERLANDS

While Sabine and Andreas were safe in England, their parents stayed in Germany to dismantle their home and business. The Fröhlich elders packed their furniture and shipped most of it to a warehouse in the port city of Bremerhaven. Georg and Edith were forced to sell their real estate below cost, and the proceeds were then confiscated by the state. The Fröhlichs also had to pay a *"Reichsfluchtsteuer,"* a huge tax extracted for the privilege of fleeing the Third Reich.

On the back of a small photo taken of Edith outside of her home on Carmerstrasse 7 she wrote, *"Abschied von Häusel Mai 1939"* (Farewell from home May 1939). The photos must have been taken just after the forced sale of their home.

In a tape recording, Edith commented on how much Georg enjoyed their house on Carmerstrasse, especially because he had resided in furnished single rooms for so many years after leaving his childhood home in Kattowitz. When they were looking for a place to buy in Breslau, Edith said George wanted a patrician home like the one in which he'd spent his childhood. Edith had more farewell photos taken at other Breslau sites. I don't know where the Fröhlichs lived from May until their exit from Germany two months later.

In 2016, my sister, brother-in-law and I visited the former Fröhlich home, now in Wrocław, Poland. It was in impressively good shape, especially considering that most of Breslau was destroyed in the last month of the war. The house to the left of Sabine's childhood home was comparatively decrepit, with pockmarks on the front that looked like bullet holes.

The Fröhlich home had been subdivided into four units. The lowest level now holds offices for an architectural firm. We walked through the large back yard with a children's slide, so perhaps a young family lives in one of the units. We were not brave enough or conversant in Polish to ring doorbells and ask to see the inside of the townhouse.

We looked for Georg's office building. It was no longer there. Instead, all we found was a falafel stand on the edge of a small shabby park surrounded by dreary utilitarian postwar buildings.

Georg and Edith had booked boat passage for their family from Bremerhaven to the United States, and hoping to join their Nissen relatives in exile. But the Fröhlichs were unable to obtain US visas. Through Dr. Rudi Nissen's connections with the Dutch ambassador in Turkey, Georg and Edith were able to obtain visas for the Netherlands. So in July they left Germany for the Netherlands, intending to stay there only temporarily while they awaited visas to the US.

As my grandfather wrote in his postwar job application to the Allied Occupation Forces:

> After my daughter had been taken up boarded [sic] with an American family in Bromley (Kent) and my son had found shelter in the college of priests at Ware, my wife and I left Germany on July 14, 1939, intending to emigrate to the USA. We got the permission for a preliminary stay in Holland thanks to the intercession of H.E. Visser, then ambassador of the Netherlands in Istanbul, and through the medium of the Minister of Justice Goseling. Here in Amsterdam we were expecting to get our summons from the USA Consul General at Rotterdam and had our children come to see us on a holiday visit.

The outbreak of war unfortunately rendered their return impossible.

In the Netherlands, the Fröhlichs first stayed in Vaals. Pater Adams became a family friend and introduced the Fröhlichs to the town's mayor, Mr. Rhoen, "because he [Adams] figured we may need some paperwork done or some permission to stay. You know, all these places, you always have to register when you come," Sabine explained.

Both Pater Adams and the mayor "were helpful in every way to my parents and me." The mayor even offered to take in some of the furniture the Fröhlichs had shipped to Holland, until they found longer-term housing. The Fröhlichs sold their grand piano and grandfather clock in Vaals to fund their living expenses.

Andreas and Sabine leave England for a Visit to Holland

The Fröhlich parents wanted their children to visit them in Holland after the English school term ended in 1939. Andreas went to the Smiths to pick up Sabine for the trip. The initial intent for the children's visit was that it be only for the summer vacation until the English school term resumed.

"That's when Andreas came and said we had to go to Holland to visit my parents. And I know we just didn't pack much stuff. We figured we'd come back. And, I think at some point, the Smiths managed to send clothing to Holland when they left for America when the war broke out. So it was a kind of saying goodbye without really imagining we wouldn't see each other again. When the Blitz started, he [Mr. Smith] took his family back to St. Louis."

When Andreas left St. Edmund's, four of his classmates wrote notes in his diary wishing him good luck upon his departure to visit his parents in Holland. These notes from his classmates are the last entries in Andreas' diary. According to St. Edmund's, three of the four classmates who signed Andreas' diary became priests.

Andreas, then 17, traveled with his sister, who was 12, to Harwich, where they boarded a boat to Hoek van Holland. From there, they took a train to Vaals to join their parents for the summer. Sabine did not have any memories of that boat trip or the reunion with her parents.

August 1939, Boarding School in Vaals

In August 1939, Edith enrolled Sabine at the Sacré Coeur Convent School for girls in Vaals. The nuns who ran the school required the students to speak French at all times, and punished the students if they were caught speaking another language. Life at the boarding school was very regimented. The convent had a dormitory, with small cubicles for rooms.

"And what I remember the most was the strict getting-up procedures," Sabine recalled. "The little bell would ring, and that would mean to get out of your bed. And then another little bell would ring and that means you take off your nightgown. And the next bell means you put on your underwear." Bells next signaled when they were to brush their teeth, comb their hair, and so on until it was time to leave for Mass.

"And we had like uniforms on, navy-blue during the week with black lace veils, and on Sundays there was white top with white lace veils. We had little veils because we were all like little nuns there. Going to mass every day was part of the procedure. When you were in a Catholic boarding school, that's what you did.

"And when we went to mass, every day, we had a stack of prayer books and song books, and everything during the mass that was sung, was sung by us. And we had Book 1, Page 90, Book 2, and so on. It was a very formal going to mass, but it was part of the procedure. You just woke up and went to mass and then you got breakfast."

Sabine remembered the Sacré Coeur School as being in a really nice building. Even though she was living in a boarding school, she could see her parents every day because the school was walking distance from where they were staying in Vaals. "They could walk over and visit, but only at certain times when classes were not scheduled. The school schedule was pretty strict. Pretty long hours of instruction, and then, of course, the sports part was instruction, and the religion part was instruction."

Sabine learned that some of the Sacré Coeur nuns were French, but others were German or Dutch. Most of the nuns spoke multiple languages, including German, because the religious order existed in many different countries.

"There was no problem with communication. I fitted in perfectly. There were a lot of children of diplomatic personnel. There was a daughter of an ambassador from South America. The population wasn't just girls from the town, it was a boarding school for families who kept moving around and couldn't take their children around everywhere because ambassadors and consuls often get reassigned. There were several nationalities there; I don't remember all of them, but they were a very international group of students.

"I do remember something that upset me was that the teachers were all called 'Mère So-and-so,' but the nuns who scrubbed the floors were called 'soeur.' And I thought it was terribly undemocratic to make a distinction between the teachers and the scrub nuns. Both worked for the glory of God. They shouldn't have been differentiated. But that's the way the order was established. It didn't seem to bother them. It bothered me.

"There was one nun I was particularly friendly with—I don't remember her name—and she asked me more about my former life and so on. But they were all very educated women. This order was either for teaching or for scrubbing. Sacré Coeur. And they still exist. And I still have a scapular of one of their saints." (A scapular is small religious necklace made of cloth with a pendant of two square wool patches.)

13

WWII STARTS, TRAPPING THE FRÖHLICHS

On September 1, 1939, Germany invaded Poland. Britain and France, standing by their treaty with Poland, declared war on Germany two days later. Poland surrendered to Germany four weeks later.

As of late summer 1939, the Fröhlich parents appear to have been undecided and ambivalent as to whether or not to send their children back to England for the fall school term. In a letter dated September 4, 1939, Mrs. Eleanor Smith wrote:

Dear Mrs. Fröhlich,

I am so full of this trouble that I can hardly write. Just this much of it has convinced me that it would be an awful thing to put the children through. I am glad indeed you have your children with you. We are sailing on the US steamer Washington on Sunday...

I know postal censorship has been established, and I don't know what I am allowed to say. The spirit here is wonderful—everyone carrying on cheerfully.

We have been busy blacking out windows and fitting up the shelter. I keep the children busy—in fact I have nearly run their legs off but it is good for them.

The packing, alone, is a tremendous job; but I am getting along well. When it is possible, I will send some at least of Sabine's and Andreas' things.

Mrs. Smith asked Edith to write back and gave her US address. She also asked for the address of Edith's brother in Boston (Dr. Rudolf Nissen who was at Massachusetts General Hospital at that time). She closed the letter with "Ever most truly your friend."

The departure of Mrs. Smith and the children for the US meant Sabine could not return to England to live with them in Bromley. Edith, however, still questioned whether Andreas should return to Ware and would be safe there.

Edith wrote to Arnold Smith asking for his opinion. In his letter on Monsanto stationery, dated September 20, 1939, Mr. Smith wrote back:

Dear Mrs. Fröhlich,

I fear that Sabina [sic] has greatly exaggerated my knowledge of German. I really only know a few words learned in school as a child—I have never spoken German at any time. So I do have considerable difficulty in reading your letters, although I probably get the main points. If you can write in English I would appreciate it very much.

Mrs. Smith and the four girls left England for the United States on the S.S. Washington on the 12th of September and should now be in New York. We got the tickets but they only were promised beds in one of the public rooms —but anyway I went to Southampton and saw them on the boat.

I would consider Ware quite a safe spot in England and if Andreas can come back I see no reason why he should not do so. It is quite possible that the situation created by the war may make a change in the plans of the Catholic Committee or the British government regulations regarding returning to this country. I do not know of any change...

I hope at a little later date to send you by some means a suitcase of Sabine's clothing. So far there is so much confusion I have been unable to do anything about it. Whenever Andreas returns he can get his things at 18 Sunridge Av. as one of our maids is staying in the house.

Sincerely,

Arnold H. Smith

Georg and Edith decided not to send either child back to England. They felt that Holland would be a safer place in wartime. Their reasoning was that Holland would stay neutral, as it had in WWI, and that Germany would not dare to invade a neutral country. The Fröhlichs were also concerned that their children would be interned as "enemy aliens" if they returned to England.[1] Edith never forgave herself for this miscalculation, which she believed cost her son's life.

The war broke out while Sabine was in the Sacré Coeur boarding school. "The nuns didn't give us any information on what was going on in the world. But one of the girls, I think, had a little radio and could tell us where they were fighting. So we knew a little bit about the war and the battles going on."

Given the Blitz, Germany's massive bombardment campaign against England during WWII, England would not necessarily have been entirely safe for Andreas. Or so I thought. When I visited St. Edmund's in 2016, however, I learned that Ware (where the college is located) was never bombed during the war.

The Sacré Coeur school became a Van der Valk hotel, Kasteel Bloemendal; the statue of St. Mary from the Catholic boarding school era stands in front of the hotel.

14

THE FRÖHLICHS MOVE TO AMSTERDAM

A few months after the start of WWII, Georg and Edith withdrew Sabine from the convent school in Vaals so she could move with them to Amsterdam. The Fröhlich parents wanted their children to live with them at a guest house called Pension Oliva while they awaited visas to join their Nissen relatives in the United States.

Years earlier, Georg had given his niece, Liesl Hohenstein, his eldest brother's daughter, money to buy property in Amsterdam to open a guest house. A condition of the gift was that if Georg ever needed to come to Holland, the niece would make rooms available for him and his family.

Pension Oliva consisted of two attractive adjacent brick buildings, four stories high, with bay windows, a small courtyard in the front and a larger courtyard in the back, edged with trees and flowering shrubs. The pension was located on Prins Hendriklaan, a street in an upscale neighborhood adjacent to Vondelpark. Andreas went to live in a room in Prins Hendriklaan 38, and the parents and Sabine lived in the building next door, Prins Hendriklaan 36.

Moving to Amsterdam meant Sabine could live with her parents again. "I wasn't unhappy to be at the boarding school, but I wasn't unhappy to leave and go to Amsterdam. That was another new adventure."

Sabine shared a furnished room with a young relative named Lillian Luley, the daughter of the Pension manager. Lillian was a little younger than Sabine. "We were not great friends, but we got along fine." Sabine described the room they shared as small and cozy. They each had a tiny bed that could be folded up.

New School and Meeting Agnes Nolte

Andreas, now 17, was enrolled in a Jesuit boys' school, St. Ignatius College. Andreas was very religious, became an acolyte at church and hoped to enter a seminary to become a priest. He made good friends at his new school.

Sabine was enrolled in a Catholic girls' school in Amsterdam run by the *Zusters Franciscanessen* (Franciscan Sisters) of Heythuysen, the name of the city where their main convent was. The school was a *Lyceum voor Meisjes* (a lyceum for girls) named the Reynier-Vinkeleskade School, after the street where the school is located. (Postwar, the school was renamed Fons Vitae Lyceum and became co-ed.)

The first time Sabine went to the Reynier-Vinkeleskade School was with her mother to meet with the principal, Sister Xaveriana, whom Sabine described as a sweet woman. The school had a rule that any new student from another country had to repeat a grade. Sabine was enrolled on November 16 after the school term had begun. It was the fourth school she'd attended, and the fourth language she'd received instruction in, this time Dutch, in the space of a year.

Sabine had a distinct recollection of the first time she entered the history class taught by Agnes Nolte. Sabine immediately noticed that the students' desks in Miss Nolte's classroom were arranged perpendicular to each other rather than in the traditional straight rows. Agnes Nolte was a dynamic teacher, with large, bright blue eyes and short, straight white hair. In a warm tone, she said to Sabine in German, "*Moment mal*" (wait just a moment), and then found a place for her to sit. This welcome in German was a simple and immensely reassuring gesture for Sabine. "She was really my main liaison with the school, and saw that I participated in everything. She immediately took me on as a ward, so to speak."

Sabine described Agnes Nolte as a "fabulous, superb teacher." "She was an absolutely marvelous teacher. I mean, there was nobody in her class who fell asleep because she would shoot questions out of the blue and point at somebody to answer. You did not go to sleep during her lessons."

The new school was about a 20-minute walk from Prins Hendriklaan. As Sabine made friends, they would meet and walk together to school. Sabine did well academically, despite having to learn in a fourth language and having to change her handwriting once again to suit the preferred style of the school. After the first year, she was ranked eighth in a class of 75. In the second year, she ranked second. (Many decades later she could recall the names of the students who placed first and third that year.)

Some of the girls that Sabine met at the Amsterdam school became her life-long friends. One was Mily Bosch. Another friend, Evie Asberg, was not originally allowed to fraternize or walk to school with Sabine because Sabine was a German. Evie would walk on one side of the street and talk to Sabine who walked along in tandem on the other side of the street. Evie asked her father, Han Asberg, to allow Sabine to visit their home so he could see for himself that she was a nice girl, and after that Evie became a close friend.

Over time, Evie's father, Han Asberg, the publisher of Urbi et Orbi, a company that printed Catholic prayer books, catechisms and other liturgical texts, became fond of Sabine, and "Tante" Jo, his wife, welcomed her as well, teaching her how to mend socks and diaper babies. Sabine spent much time at the busy Asberg house, playing games with the children (Evie was one of 13 siblings) and helping out.

Han Asberg would later risk his life more than once to help the Fröhlich family, by creating false papers and finding them hiding places.

PHOTOS

Nissen Surgical Clinic, Neisse (circa 1910)

Edith Nissen (circa 1915)

Georg Fröhlich (circa 1917)

Dr. Franz Nissen reading on balcony of Nissen Surgical Clinic (circa 1920)

Edith Fröhlich Nissen and Andreas (1922)

Edith, Andreas and Sabine in Zuppot (1928)

Edith and Georg (circa 1930)

Andreas and Sabine, Breslau (1934)

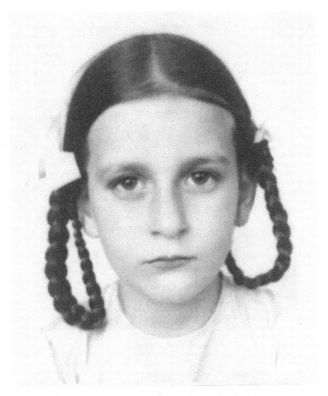

Sabine (1935)

Biedermeierzimmer at Carmerstrasse 7 in Breslau

Andreas, Edith, Sabine, Breslau (1938)

Sabine leaving for Kindertransport. L-R: Edith, Frau Schwartzer,
Sabine and Frau Emma (January 1939)

Sabine's German passport (January 1939)

Andreas, Edith, Pater Adams, and Sabine in Vaals (1939)

Andreas and Sabine, Prins Hendriklaan 36 Amsterdam (circa 1940)

Sabine playing with Willy Corsari's cats (1940)

Andreas's last photo, age 19 (May 1941)

Agnes Nolte (R) with sisters Roos (center) and Mies (date unknown)

Han and Tante Jo Asberg

*Klaas and Maria E. Schipper family. L-R: Cor, Klaas, Ali, Annie,
Maria E., Afra (mid-1920s)*

*Schippers Hoogkarspel N.H. Standing (L-R): Kees, Arie, Klaas, Jan,
Cor, Piet, Dirk, sitting, Trien, Guurtje, Gre, Aagje, Katrien (May
1939)*

*Schipper Family Hoogkarspel. L-R: Ali, Afra, Maria Elizabeth,
Annie, Cor, Klaas (circa 1925)*

Cor in Dutch military uniform (circa 1940)

Sabine with the Schapers in front of their store in Hoogkarspel (postwar).

Jan and Johanna Elders, rescuers for last hiding place of where Fröhlichs were reunited (postwar)

Sabine and Cor (postwar)

Sabine holding school flag on Liberation Day Parade, (1945) Courtesy of Aad
Streefland

15

THE GERMANS INVADE, ANDREAS MURDERED IN MAUTHAUSEN

On May 10, 1940, the Germans launched their invasion of Belgium, Luxembourg and the Netherlands. The Dutch were forced to surrender in five days. A few days later, Sabine watched the Germans enter Amsterdam marching and singing, accompanied by trucks and tanks. The Germans wore green, and the Dutch Nazis wore black and red uniforms. Sabine remembered that nearly everyone watching the Germans was silent, except for some cheers from a few Dutch Nazis.

"They marched and marched, so well and so precise," Sabine recalled. The display gave her a life-long antipathy toward perfect military marching. She commented that she felt relief when watching typical Memorial Day parades in the United States because the marching was so poor.

In the winter and spring after the German invasion, all persons of Jewish origin were required to register with the Joodse Raad, the Jewish governing council set up by the Nazis. Each Jewish person was assigned a number based on various categories including percentage of Jewish ancestry.

The Fröhlichs believed they received a relatively high *stempel* (stamp) number because they were Catholic rather than practicing Jews and because Georg was a German war veteran. The Fröhlichs also believed that registering with the Joodse Raad would help protect the family. More importantly, they had to be registered to obtain exit visas to emigrate. As with the rest of her family, Sabine's Dutch identification papers were stamped with a large "J" for Jewish ancestry.

As Catholics, the Fröhlichs had no connection with the local Jewish community in Amsterdam, but did have connections with other refugees. Between 1930 and 1940, some 34,000 Germans of Jewish ancestry emigrated to the Netherlands. Refugee Jews lived all over Amsterdam, wherever they could afford the housing. Amsterdam Jews of lower income lived in a mostly Jewish area called Waterlooplein. More affluent Jews, including Anne Frank's family before going into hiding, settled in the Rivierenbuurt, where the streets were named after rivers. Pension Oliva where the Fröhlichs and several other Jewish refugees stayed was just east of the Rivierenbuurt, in the well-off neighborhood of Oud-Zuid, adjacent to Vondelpark and a short walking distance to Museumplein.

One of the non-Jewish pension residents was Willy Corsari, pseudonym for Wilhelmina A. Douwes-Schmidt, the well-known Dutch writer of novels, short stories, detective tales and plays. Willy Corsari was a pleasant and engaging eccentric who lived with her mother and five Siamese cats on an upper floor. Sabine enjoyed spending time in Willy's apartment, as attested by several photographs in which she is playing with the author's Siamese cats. Willy could charm people, including the police who later came to arrest boarders at the pension. She was helpful to the Fröhlichs, hiding family papers, jewelry and photographs for them.

In February 1941, members of a Jewish youth group fought with the Dutch police and one policeman was injured. In retaliation, the Gestapo arrested some 300 young Jewish men and transported them first to Schoorl, a holding camp in Holland, and from there deported them to Buchenwald concentration camp. It was the first *razzia*, a mass roundup and arrest of Jews. None of the boys came back. The whole country went on strike, Sabine recalled, to protest. For two days, nothing ran—no trams, no buses, nothing. The Nazis threatened to treat the Jews even more harshly if the strike continued. It stopped. However, from February until June 1941, there were no mass arrests and deportation of Jews.

In the meanwhile, the German occupiers commissioned Amsterdam municipal officials to create a map identifying the location of all Jewish residents of the city, based on mandated registrations. The very efficient city functionaries generated a large map (100 centimeters square or over three feet square) in May 1941 titled, "*Verspreiding van de Joden over de Gemeente*" (Distribution of Jews over the Municipality). Each dot on the big map represented the street by street location of 10 Jews.[1]

The Nazi restrictions and humiliations that the Fröhlichs had experienced in Breslau and sought to escape now methodically resurfaced in the Netherlands in 1941. "Jews not Welcome" signs began appearing in front of restaurants and coffee houses. Next, "Jews Forbidden" signs at cinemas, theaters, public reading and meeting rooms, and swimming pools. In April 1941, all orchestras were made "*Judenfrei*" (Jew free). The next month, Jews were banned from beaches and beach boulevards, bathing houses, public parks, botanical gardens and zoos. In subsequent months, the bans were extended to train station waiting rooms, sleeping and restaurant cars on trains, hotels, libraries and museums, sporting events, artistic performances and concerts.[2]

In early June 1941, a bomb damaged a German marine officers' club in Amsterdam. Another bomb at the Luftwaffe's telephone exchange at Schiphol seriously injured a soldier. The Dutch Resistance had likely set off the bombs.

On June 11, 1941, Georg Fröhlich left the Pension early and boarded a tram for the central train station. He then took a train to The Hague, where he planned to visit the Consulate of Ecuador, hoping to obtain exit visas for his family. Georg had made a connection with M. Utrero Gomez, the General Consul of Ecuador in Holland, through the

Heinemans' brother-in-law, Fritz. Fritz, who lived in Quito and knew the Gomez children, had recommended that the Fröhlichs travel to Ecuador and stay there until they could emigrate to the United States.

The Fröhlichs had prepaid transatlantic boat fares, but after two years had still not been able to obtain visas to the United States. Mr. Gomez said he would grant Georg and his family the long-sought transit visas to Ecuador. He would also write a letter to the Consuls of Spain, Portugal and Cuba, asking them to facilitate the emigration of "Dr. Jona Froehlich, ex-government counselor, his wife and two children, to the United States of America, where Dr. Rodolfo Nissen, famous professor and surgeon, and brother-in-law of Dr. Froehlich, has taken all the necessary steps and presented all the guarantees for the case." (Jona is a version of Jonas, Georg's middle name.)

Sabine remembers it was a warm, dry June day. For her, it began as an ordinary school day. While Georg was in The Hague and she was at school, Edith left the Pension. Sabine is not sure why her mother left —perhaps to visit friends, run errands or go shopping.

Neither parent was at the Pension Oliva that afternoon when Sabine walked home from school. Two young men in plain clothes were standing at the doorway to Prins Hendriklaan 36 when she arrived. The young men watched her go inside the Pension, where she continued on to her parents' room.

The young men followed her, knocked on the door of Georg and Edith's room, and asked for Andreas Fröhlich. Sabine thought they might be people from church, from the 'Congregation' youth group at Obrechtkerk, a group of acolytes her brother belonged to. To her, the men appeared to be about her brother's age. She told the young men that Andreas lived next door (at Prins Hendriklaan 38) and that "*Ik weet niet of hij thuis is*" (I don't know if he's home).

She went to the Pension building next door and the young men followed her. They went through the small front courtyard and down to the lower level where there was a kitchen. The young men asked the kitchen employees, "Is Andreas home?" They shook their heads and answered, "No." The kitchen staff gave Sabine a look she could not interpret. She said to the young men, "*Maar daar staat zijn fiets.*" (But his bike is here).

Sabine was 14 years old; no-one had taught her other than to tell the truth. "They went up and got him." The young men went upstairs to Andreas' room and arrested him. They told her that Andreas had to go to Euterpestraat with them. And that is when she first began to understand was happening. Euterpe Street, named after the Greek goddess of music and lyric poetry, was the location of Gestapo headquarters. The young men were Dutch police agents in civilian clothes working for the Gestapo.

Had the young men worn the uniforms of the *Grüne Polizei*, Sabine commented repeatedly over the years, then she would have recognized that they were the police. "But they were dressed in regular clothes. They asked for him by name."

"When I came home from school, somebody should have warned me, but they didn't. That was the big mistake," she said, "because Andreas could have easily escaped over the rooftops as other young men did. It's gnawed at me my whole life."

Shortly after Andreas was arrested, Edith arrived back at the Pension; she was frantic. By then, she had heard rumors that the Gestapo was picking up young Jewish men all around Amsterdam, and she had rushed back home. Agents for the Gestapo were rounding up so-called "suspects" for acts of sabotage carried out by the Dutch Resistance earlier in June. The full import of the roundup, however, was not immediately clear. No one knew what would happen to the arrested boys.

Edith went directly to Gestapo headquarters on Euterpe Street for information about her son. Andreas had been taken there, but Edith was not allowed to see him. Edith was told to bring a toothbrush and some nightclothes for Andreas, which she did. Georg later arrived at the Pension with the long-awaited news about exit visas. But now it was too late. The Fröhlichs did not want to leave Holland without their son.

Andreas was one of about 300 innocent men, aged 18 to 20, rounded up by the Gestapo from June 11 to 13. This particular *razzia* targeted German-Jewish refugees. Another boy picked up in the same *razzia* as Andreas was Peter Loeser, the son of a Breslau lawyer who was a friend of the Fröhlichs. Peter saw Andreas at Gestapo headquarters in Amsterdam but was not allowed to talk to him.

At first, the Fröhlichs thought that Andreas would only be gone for a few days. A few days later, they learned that the boys who had been picked up had been taken from Gestapo headquarters to a temporary camp for "picked up" people in Schoorl, close to Bergen, in the dune country on the North Sea.

When the Fröhlichs and other families learned their boys were at Schoorl, they thought they were being taken for *Arbeitsdienst* or conscripted work service in a factory, a mandatory service for boys in Germany in their first year after high school graduation. The Schoorl camp was a Dutch army camp that the Nazis had converted into a prison camp. The camp administration did not notify the Fröhlichs or any other parents that their sons had been transferred there. The information instead came via word of mouth from the Joodse Raad.

Mauthausen

Andreas stayed at Schoorl for only two days. He was then sent to two other *Durchgangslager* (transit or holding camps), Vught and Westerbork. Ultimately, Andreas and the other boys were transferred to the Mauthausen concentration camp in Austria. Peter was lucky; he was the last of five boys released from Gestapo custody because of "ill health" before the transfer to Mauthausen. (Peter went into hiding, survived the war and emigrated to the US.)

We now know from Mauthausen records that Andreas arrived at the concentration camp on June 23, less than two weeks after the roundups in Amsterdam. He was registered as Lot Fröhlich, Prisoner

No. 1983, Lot being the Nazi-imposed name. He was treated as a political prisoner because he was deemed Jewish under Nazi laws and therefore considered an enemy of the Third Reich.

The Fröhlichs learned that Andreas had been sent to Mauthausen through the Joodse Raad. Edith went to the Gestapo chiefs in Amsterdam, Willy Lages and Ferdinand aus der Fünten, and pleaded with them to release her son. She gave them jewels and cash, and they promised to get Andreas out of Mauthausen. The promise was empty, a deliberate extortion or trick. Lages and aus der Fünten were the two top Nazis in charge of the Jewish liquidation in Amsterdam. (They were convicted and sentenced to life in prison after the war, but both were released early.)

Sabine said that her parents were aware that Mauthausen was a concentration camp, but that that did not mean much initially. The Fröhlichs knew some people had been sent to Dachau and other camps, beaten and then released. They knew concentration camps were a punishment colony and that people were mistreated there, but few (other than Nazis) knew then about the existence of death- or extermination camps. Then the first batch of death notices began arriving at the Joodse Raad from Mauthausen on boys picked up in the first *razzia* of February 1941.

Andreas wrote two letters to his family while he was at Mauthausen. "We had to be very careful what we wrote and he had to be careful what he wrote," Sabine said. Andreas' letters were written on pre-printed forms and were heavily censored, with big portions blacked out. The letters arrived about midway during Andreas' imprisonment. Sabine said the letters gave no information about camp conditions and were taken as "just a sign of life."

Sabine wrote to Andreas that she was taking Latin and Greek at school and that she hoped that he would come back and help her with her homework. In his second and last letter, Andreas wrote back, "*Sabine wird ihre Schularbeiten allein machen müssen*" (Sabine will have to do her homework herself). Her family understood right away that Andreas knew he was going to die. Sabine did not save the two letters because it became too dangerous to keep them later in the war when she went into hiding.

Death notices from Mauthausen began to arrive regularly at the Joodse Raad, initially for the boys arrested in the first *razzia*, then for the boys picked up in the second *razzia*, more and more notices every day. Often no reason was given for the death, just the fact of death. If a reason for death was given, it was one of three: *Lungenentzündung* (pneumonia), *auf der Flucht erschossen* (shot while fleeing), or *Freitod* (suicide).

Edith could not bring herself to go to the Joodse Raad and read the death lists. Tante Bella Dispeker, a tiny lady in her seventies, went every day to look at the death notices on her behalf. Bella, a Jewish refugee from Bavaria, was a friend of the Fröhlichs. One day in mid-November, about five months after Andreas had been picked up, Tante Bella came up the stairs to the Fröhlichs' room and told them, "He's on it."

The Mauthausen concentration camp's gruesome history, atrocious conditions and barbaric treatment of prisoners are well documented and were described earlier. Only eight of about 900 young men sent from the Netherlands to Mauthausen in 1941 survived to the end of the year, a 99 percent mortality rate, and not one lived to see liberation. The camp's death register listing the cause of Andreas' death as *Lungenentzündung, Kreislaufschwäche* (pneumonia, circulatory weakness) was almost certainly a fabrication. Even the date and time recorded for his death are questionable. We do not know what happened to Andreas at Mauthausen or how he died. We know only that he was operated on, the fact of his death and that Andreas knew he was doomed before he died.

16

NAZI RESTRICTIONS ON JEWS TIGHTEN

After Andreas was rounded up, the Fröhlichs set up a hiding place for Sabine in the Pension on Prins Hendriklaan 36. Whenever strangers came to the door, Sabine was to hide in an alcove above the portico over the entrance to the boarding house. Edith and Georg timed Sabine to see how quickly and quietly she could climb up along the protruding ridges of the leaded windows to reach her *schuilplaats* (hiding place). She had to position herself so that she would not be visible from outside or inside the building. Sabine described it as an "excellent hiding place."

Sabine also had to learn to make the bed in her room quickly and neatly because if Gestapo agents found a warm, unmade bed, they would know that she was still in the Pension or not far away. Sabine spent a number of nights sleeping in the alcove above the front door when rumors spread about Gestapo roundups.

"They put a small mattress in there, a couple of blankets, some pillows and some books, and that was my private place. And when the doorbell rang at night, I was always afraid they were coming for my parents. They did come for somebody and picked him up. I remember that, but I don't remember his name."

Sabine's school friends who came to visit her thought the alcove was a neat arrangement and enjoyed spending time with her up there. Sometime after Andreas was picked up in the *razzia* but before the Fröhlichs learned he had perished, the principal of Sabine's school died. "I went to Sister Xaveriana's funeral and cried my eyes out," Sabine recalled.

Restrictions tighten

The restrictions on Jews now extended to a curfew at 8 p.m. and tightened relentlessly. The Jewish residents at the Pension Oliva began getting knocks on the door at 8 p.m. to check whether they had complied with the curfew. In December 1941, Jews were banned from non-Jewish schools. Hence, at age 14—a few weeks before her 15th birthday—Sabine was forced again to leave her Catholic school. She remembered this as a very, very bitter moment in her life.

Sabine tried to keep up with her classes by learning at home. In early 1942, she was permitted to go to her school once a week for some private instruction, and her school friends brought her homework every day. Learning in this manner was more difficult, and only partially successful, she said.

Later on, however, she could not go to the school at all, even after hours for tutoring. At significant risk, Agnes Nolte privately tutored Sabine in her own apartment, and gave her homework from her other teachers. There was a Jewish school in Amsterdam, but Sabine did not attend that school. Raised as a Catholic, she did not feel she had much in common with the Jewish students, nor was she familiar with the Jewish school.

In the spring of 1942, the Germans suddenly evicted all residents of the second house of the Pension, Prins Hendriklaan 38, to make room for families of the German occupation forces. The kitchen was in that building. Sabine had no experience with cooking.

"I hardly knew when water was boiling or when potatoes and vegetables were done. Also, we had no cooking equipment, only an electric hot plate which we could not use because of the high electric [wattage] use and cost. And also, except for water, everything on the hot plate burned." With great effort, the Fröhlichs were able to obtain a few pots, pans and utensils, items Jews could only buy with difficulty.

Willy Corsari, the author who lived above the Fröhlichs, allowed them to use her gas cooker with two burners, as did as the Luleys, who lived a floor below and owned a cooker with three burners. Ration cards and a web of restrictions made shopping for food complicated and arduous. Georg did much of the shopping, being better able to navigate through the multiple restrictions and befriend store personnel.

Gestapo laws allowed Jews to shop only between 3 p.m. and 5 p.m., times when the stores were already crowded. The Fröhlichs were only permitted to buy vegetables at a store half an hour away, and then, very often, after being in line for three hours, they were unable to buy anything. Sabine had to learn to cook, running up and down stairs with the small, assembled collection of cooking utensils to heat and monitor meals. Meals burned or grew cold when Miss Corsari took the Fröhlichs' pots off the burner to cook something for herself.

"I remember well when I was not home one day and had asked Muti [mother] to watch the peas which were cooking two floors above us. When I returned, Muti had company and when I enquired after my peas, she screamed. So I knew enough already, and we raced up the stairs. As you can imagine, peas black, pot black and a terrible smell. I was a dejected cook and no vegetables for dinner."

Sabine found running a household this way was difficult, time consuming and tedious. And she very much missed school and learning.

Spring-Summer 1942: Yellow Stars and the "Abholungen"

Sabine described the cooking misadventures as "a few of the small annoyances" until the spring and summer of 1942 when the Nazi segregation measures and terror against Jews intensified. "That is when we got the stars and the *Abholungen* began," she said. The literal meaning of the term *Abholungen* is pickups or collection. In reality, *Abholungen* meant mass roundups of Jews for transport to the concentration camps.

Beginning on April 29, 1942, Jews were forced to wear yellow, six-pointed stars of David with the word *Jood* (Jew) printed in the center. The Joodse Raad distributed the patches, and only one or two stars were allotted per person to stitch on outer clothing. Sabine said that everyone had to be very careful with the stitching because the stars were made out of very cheap material and ripped easily.

From the curfew to the wearing of yellow stars of David, restrictions intensified. Jews were not allowed to go to the movies, or to public theaters, except one, the Hollandsche Schouwburg, which became a Jewish theater. Later in the war, the theater itself became a holding area for Jews before transport to Westerbork, and then on to concentration camps.

Later, Jews were not allowed to use public transportation. "At some point, we couldn't go on the tram," Sabine recalled. Jews could not own bikes. Jews could only shop in Jewish stores and buy from Jewish butchers and bakers. Jews could only go to Jewish hospitals. Sabine was not allowed to visit non-Jewish houses, so she could no longer legally visit her friends.

Between July 1942 and July 1943, around 60,000 Jews were deported from Amsterdam. The Dutch municipal administration, police and railway workers assisted in the round-ups and transport of Jews. Members of the Joodse Raad ended up functioning as involuntary collaborators with the Nazis in the liquidation of Jews. When the Nazis wanted to collect so-called workers for transport to so-called labor camps, they would demand the Joodse Raad select 1,000 Jews (or some other number) to be brought to a roundup point or train station, which the Raad would do—presumably sparing their own families. The Nazis threatened Jews who refused to report for the so-called labor service with deportation to Mauthausen, by then well known in the Netherlands as the site of a particularly brutal death camp. In the end, however, members of the Joodse Raad themselves were sent to concentration camps in Theresienstadt—or worse.

17

SABINE IN HIDING, EDITH'S ARREST

During 1942, Han Asberg took a great risk to pick up Sabine at home and cover her yellow star with his hand as they walked or went on his bicycle to the Asberg home so she could visit her friend Evie and the rest of the Asberg family. Mr. Asberg became concerned that life in Amsterdam was growing too perilous for Sabine. He began making elaborate plans for her to hide in a convent outside of the city. He was in the publishing business and owned a printing press, so he could create official looking documents.

"Mr. Asberg thought it was becoming so dangerous," Sabine recalled, "that he made plans to let me 'disappear.' He took care of false papers for me, where I was called Liesje Schmidt, born in Medan, Netherlands East Indies, with a birth certificate he had printed in his printing press. It turned out very well."

Mr. Asberg also created a history for Liesje that Sabine had to memorize: "A whole novel was put together, which more or less said that I, Liesje, was born in Medan and went to school in Padang with the sisters of one of the largest Dutch order of nuns, the *Zusters van Liefde* (Sisters of Charity). And then in 1939, to complete my studies, I traveled to Holland with my mother. While we were visiting friends in Ostend, Belgium, my mother wanted to go to England for a few days to visit friends. She left me, Liesje, with friends [in Belgium] but since war broke out in those days with Holland, she could not come back.

"So the friends brought me to Holland to an aunt, for which a sister-in-law of Asberg played the role. Then I lived two more years in Amsterdam. But by July 1942, I was looking so unwell, that it was decided to send me to the countryside for a while.

"Herr Asberg had a relative at the Mother House of this order of nuns, which also had a school in Padang. Through this connection [the relative], he came into contact with the right hand of the Mother Superior General, a Sister Johanna, who bought into our case and was told about the plan with Liesje Schmidt. Sister Johanna wanted to help. She asked Mother Superior for permission because if this [ruse for sheltering a Jew] was ever uncovered, these nuns would be put out of their more than 100 buildings in Holland. The Mother Superior took the position that she did not have to know anything about Sabine Fröhlich, but had only heard that a girl from Indonesia, by the name of Liesje Schmidt, would like to come into one of her houses [convents] in the country to convalesce. And for that that, she gave her permission.

"So an official exchange of letters was put together between Mr. Van der Hoek [alias for Asberg] and his sister-in-law, who then brought me to the nun's convent in Budel, near Eindhoven, where the sisters already had gotten the news that a girl from Indonesia would come for a few months to recover. Not one person in the whole convent knew the real state of affairs. Not even the rector and the local Mother Superior."

At the convent, the nuns fed Liesje a liter of milk a day and "I was fattened up." The local rector was curious about the reasons for her stay at the convent. "The rector asked a lot of questions in the beginning, and probably came to the conclusion that my parents didn't get along very well, since he often asked if I had not witnessed differences of opinion or fights between my parents. I left him with this delusion and kept playing the role."

Playing the role included her reaction to cool weather. "I was always freezing because in my home in Indonesia it was always such wonderful temperatures." Sabine said the nuns were very kind to her, practically adopting Liesje.

During the day, she assisted the nuns in the school. She learned Malay to become more like an Indonesian, but insisted that her family always spoke English at home and she read English books "for show." She also kept busy with 11 children who had been orphaned and were being raised by the nuns.

"When I walked in the village, the children called me from all sides, *Juffrouw* (Miss) Liesje, because they had to call me that name in school." In the paperwork Mr. Asberg made Sabine two years younger than her actual age, "otherwise I would have had to have an identity card with photo and fingerprints, and that was not obtainable at the time. Therefore, I was 13 years old."

Mr. Asberg visited Sabine a few times at the convent. Sabine's parents, however, did not because they did not know where she was hiding—for her own safety.

Edith Fröhlich Arrested

In late July 1942, while Sabine was hiding at the Budel convent, the Dutch Catholic Bishops Conference published a strongly worded letter condemning the persecution of Jews. The anti-Nazi letter was read from the pulpits at all parishes. In retaliation, Arthur Seyss-Inquart, the Reich's Commissar of the Netherlands, ordered a mass arrest of Jewish converts on August 2.

Edith was baptized when she converted to Catholicism as a young adult and had her two children baptized, so all three were registered as Jewish converts with the Joodse Raad. A German policeman (*Grüne Polizei*) came to Pension Oliva to arrest Edith and Sabine.

Georg's name was not on the policeman's list because he was not baptized when he registered with the Joodse Raad. He converted to

Catholicism sometime after Andreas' death because he wanted to be part of the religion that was so important to his son and as a source of comfort to his wife. Georg had also been given a *stempel* (stamp) on his registration noting his German war service. This stamp gave him a different status, marking him out for more preferential treatment. These are the likely reasons Georg was not ordered to be arrested at the same time as his baptized wife and daughter.

Georg and Edith told the policeman that their daughter was dead. There was no way for the policeman to immediately check this story. Edith was arrested. The policeman took Edith to the trolley station and they boarded a tram. The destination was a train station where baptized Jews were being collected for transport to concentration camps. On that day, the train stations where Jews were being assembled were in Amersfoort, southeast of Amsterdam, and Westerbork in the province of Drenthe in the north of the Netherlands.

In the trolley car on the way to the train station, Edith faked a heart attack. The policeman took Edith off the trolley car and went with her to a doctor's office. The doctor declared that "the woman is dying." The policeman left, and Edith eventually went home from the doctor's office.[1] Georg and Edith left the Pension for a few days for their own safety. Sabine did not know where they stayed those days; she was in the Budel convent.

The Nazis arrested many Jewish-born priests and nuns in this *razzia*. One was Edith Stein, a Jew from Breslau who had converted to Catholicism. (The Fröhlich parents knew of the Stein family from their Breslau days.) Edith Stein had become a nun, taking the name of Sister Benedicta of the Cross, and a well-known author. The Carmelite order of nuns sent her from Germany to the Netherlands in 1938 for her safety. Arrested on August 2, Edith Stein and her sister Rosa were transported to Auschwitz and immediately gassed. (The Catholic Church beatified Edith as a martyr in 1987 and canonized her as a saint in 1998.)

18

RETURN TO AMSTERDAM, THE "WORST TIME"

Not long after the aborted arrest of Edith, Georg thought that he had everything in order for his family to leave the Netherlands and go to America via Spain. But for this departure to occur, it was necessary that Sabine become legal again because of possible checks into her background. As a non-Aryan, she had to be at home for the 8 p.m. curfew.

After four months at the convent in Budel, Liesje had to become Sabine again, and to show up in Amsterdam with a Jewish star and her identity card with the "J" on it. The Fröhlichs notified Han Asberg that they needed him to retrieve their daughter so that they could leave together for Spain. Han Asberg arrived at the convent in November 1942 and took Sabine back to Amsterdam. Sabine did not know what story Mr. Asberg gave the nuns to explain Liesje's sudden departure from their convent.

The next months in Amsterdam, the winter of 1942 and spring of 1943, were the worst part of the war for the family. "That time—waiting for the exit visas—was the most terrible time because a lot of deportations were going on," Sabine told me. Unfortunately, the trip via Spain fell apart, and the Fröhlichs remained trapped in the Netherlands.

Sabine described those times of constant terror in a letter to her Nissen uncles:

> *You were always in fear: on the street, every time the doorbell rang, but above all, in the evenings and nights. Every car passing by, every step we heard, all was listened to in fear. All our good friends had specific ways to ring the bell and when the bell rang normally, we didn't open the door. You could always be picked up. Those were the so-called S or Strafffalle (punishment cases). Those came through denouncements.*
>
> *Or there could be a house search. Fish, eggs and fruit we were not allowed to have. And when we had gotten something like this as a present, it was quickly eaten and the leftovers carefully put into an Aryan garbage can at the house.*

The Gestapo arrested Jews based on denouncements from neighbors for transgressions of the restrictions. The Gestapo also arrested Jews if any items forbidden to Jews were found during a house search. "Every day, there were new horror stories, but they were mostly all too true. Good friends disappeared. Here and there some went into hiding. There was always something going on."

A second false birth certificate was made for Sabine in the name of Christine Benit, the maiden name of Willy Corsari's mother. In this story, Sabine was the illegitimate daughter of Miss Corsari, a plausible story for an eccentric female author. Sabine had to memorize Christine's birthday and a new life history. The Christine Benit birth certificate was in case of an emergency.

Sabine kept in contact with her school friends, two of whom, Evie Asberg and Mily Bosch, visited her daily, carrying news from her school. Her friends brought her books from the library, where she and those deemed Jews were no longer allowed, and kept her company for many hours. Sabine's parents dispersed almost all their belongings to their friends so that if they were picked up by the Gestapo, at least something would be saved. Sabine's friends safeguarded her musical instruments, books and toys. But even giving away belongings was dangerous because Germans living in the neighborhood might notice suitcases being removed from the Pension Oliva and denounce the Fröhlichs.

Andreas' friends visited the Fröhlichs on a regular basis, and sometimes came after dark to take smaller boxes of belongings away. Unfortunately, many of these dispersed belongings were never recovered because they were lost or stolen during the later years of the German occupation.

The Fröhlichs become the Schmidts

Living in Amsterdam became constantly more dangerous. Nothing progressed with the Fröhlichs' exit papers and the situation was becoming increasingly desperate. So Mr. Asberg made yet another effort to manufacture new documentation, this time for Edith and Georg.

Creating a new story and new papers for the Fröhlich parents was much more complicated because they did not speak Dutch very well. Sabine described Han Asberg as "incredible" for the risks he took. She told me that she believed that Mr. Asberg, a devout Catholic, saw it as his religious duty to protect her and her family.

Mr. Asberg composed "another novella," Sabine wrote to her uncles. This time the story was about a couple who were born in Indonesia, but had always lived in Germany, and had come to Holland after a bombardment. Edith and Georg Fröhlich were renamed Herr and Frau Schmidt.

"By the sweat of their brows," Sabine wrote, her parents learned the Schmidts' birth dates, as well as the birth dates of their fictional parents and grandparents, and their Indonesian birthplaces. With this information memorized, Herr and Frau Schmidt went to the Amsterdam *Bevolkingsregister* (Dutch residents registry) to obtain papers. An official there was in on the Schmidt story so that the Schmidts could receive fake identity cards "based on the somewhat believable story."

The questioning of the Schmidts went reasonably well at the registry until Edith suffered a memory lapse: she could not remember the birth date and birthplace of her fictional grandmother. Edith pretended to have a sudden fainting spell, diverting the questioner's attention. The Fröhlichs returned home as the Schmidts without wearing their yellow stars or carrying their official identity cards—a dangerous risk.

The "Schmidts" had to provide the Dutch registry with their address in Amsterdam. They used the address of Frau Mathias, a German woman who worked at the Pension Oliva as a cook. Frau Mathias had helped the Fröhlichs obtain food during the winter and kept some of the Fröhlichs' belongings for safekeeping (a fur coat, down comforters and cooking utensils). The statements that the Schmidts made at the registry in Amsterdam were forwarded to the Central *Bevolkingsregister* in The Hague. There an official became suspicious about the Indonesia story, and sent an investigator to Amsterdam.

The investigator visited the home of Frau Mathias (whose address the Fröhlichs had listed as theirs) and asked her about the Schmidts. Frau Mathias faithfully told the investigator what she had been instructed to say in case of an investigation. But then Georg was summoned to report to the chief investigator in The Hague to give more information. That, of course, would be impossible. Georg did not feel the Indonesian Schmidt story would hold up under intense questioning and scrutiny.

Georg, Edith and Sabine left the Pension that night with their Schmidt papers in hand. They rode for hours on a trolley car, uncertain of what to do next and fearful for their future. Sabine became sick, so the Fröhlich parents took her to the home of a teacher who accepted her with great cordiality.

Eventually, Georg and Edith returned to their room at the Pension, where they discovered that other residents had used the opportunity to steal what they could of what little remained of the Fröhlichs' belongings. With much trouble, Georg and Edith were able to recover some of their belongings. Three weeks later, her parents allowed Sabine to come back home.

When the doorbell rang at night, Miss Corsari opened the door. Miss Corsari was very pretty, spoke German fluently, and could chat up and sweet-talk with the Gestapo agents. But it didn't help much. The Gestapo police came to the Pension Oliva two more times.

One time, Sabine recalled, the Gestapo came and arrested Dr. Manheimer, a professor from Berlin who lived at the Pension. He was brought to the Joodsche Schouwburg where Jews were being gathered and held for transport to the Westerbork transit camp and from there to be transferred to concentration camps. The day after his arrest, Dr. Manheimer jumped out of a window on an upper floor of the theater, killing himself. After his death, windows at the rear and sides of the Schouwburg were blocked.[1]

"Suicides took place constantly," Sabine wrote. "Zyankali (cyanide) was the most desired article," i.e. poison of choice.

On another occasion, the Gestapo came for a man who had not lived at the Pension for some time. During both instances when the Gestapo came, Sabine hid in the alcove. From above the front door, she listened carefully and fearfully to the conversations below because the Gestapo could have come to seize her or her parents.

One night, the son of Frau Mathias, the woman whose address the Fröhlichs had used for the fictitious Schmidts' address, came to Mr. Asberg's home. The son told Mr. Asberg that another investigator had come to his mother's home, but that this time, his mother had been forced to give the inspector the real names and address of the Fröhlichs.

Mr. Asberg quickly manufactured a new set of false identity papers for the Fröhlichs. These papers were not of good quality, but had to suffice. Sabine, Georg and Edith had to learn yet another set of names, birthdays and life histories. This time, the Fröhlichs were named Gerard, Elizabeth and Sophie Fredericks, names chosen to match the initials marked on some of their clothing.

The Fröhlichs made plans to go into hiding in the Dutch countryside. A friend of Andreas', Rob Wagenaar, made the first contacts with the underground in North Holland on behalf of the Fröhlichs.

19

SABINE HOSPITALIZED, HIDES IN AGNES NOLTE'S ATTIC

In the early summer of 1943, Sabine had an appendectomy, a prophylactic operation. Sabine had experienced episodes of sharp abdominal pains indicative of attacks of appendicitis. An acute attack of appendicitis during a time of hiding would have been impossibly dangerous. The operation was carried out at a Jewish hospital, the CIS (*Centraal Israelitisch Ziekenhuis*), located near the Reynier-Vinkeleskade School.

Sabine was supposed to stay in the hospital for several days after the appendectomy until the staples were ready to come out. However, her parents learned that the Germans were planning to empty out the CIS. Although Sabine could barely stand with the pain, her parents removed her from the hospital at night, and took her to the office of an elderly doctor, Ruysch van Dugteren, who was Agnes Nolte's doctor. Sabine stayed with the elderly doctor for one night. She believes this doctor removed the staples.

The next day, Agnes Nolte brought Sabine to her apartment on Quinten Massijsstraat 8 in South Amsterdam. Sabine was still bedridden, with pain and severe cramps. The rumors about the CIS hospital proved true. The Nazis later emptied out the hospital and deported all the patients to concentration camps.

Unable to return to the Pension Oliva, Georg and Edith stayed with friends in The Hague until a safer hiding place was found in September 1943 on a farm in Zwaagdijk in North Holland. After the Fröhlich parents fled Amsterdam, the Gestapo came searching for Georg, with his name and photograph on a wanted list.

Sabine was convinced she and her parents would not have lived through the German occupation without the underground contacts made by Andreas' friends. Sabine recalled, "Andreas was an acolyte at the Obrecht Kerk, it is a higher rank than altar boy for the older young men. One of his friends, Rob Wagenaar, joined the Resistance. He came to us and said I had to go into hiding, and he found hiding places for my parents and me... Without that connection to the underground, we may not have survived."

Sabine stayed with her teacher, whom she now called *Tante* (Aunt) Agnes, for three months after Georg and Edith left Amsterdam to hide in The Hague and then in the Dutch countryside. Agnes Nolte lived with her mother and sister, Roos, on two floors of an Amsterdam apartment building, Quinten-Massijsstraat 8. Sabine lived in an attic room above Ms. Nolte's apartment. When the doorbell rang, Sabine hid in the attic, as she was not allowed to be seen by anyone who lived outside the building. Whenever the doorbell rang, she would "disappear" upstairs.

Tante Agnes' sister Roos was also a teacher, who commuted to her job in Volendam via a ferry. Because Sabine had no ration card, the Noltes had to find ways to obtain food for her. Roos would obtain *paling* (smoked eel, a Dutch delicacy), cheese and other edibles in Volendam and then hide the food under her coat on her way back home. This was risky because police often met ferries as they arrived in Amsterdam and asked passengers to open their coats and drop all belongings as they disembarked. Fortunately, Roos was a buxom woman who could hide food on her body, and was never caught with the illegal provisions.

While Roos and Agnes were away teaching, Sabine would read, knit, sew and play cards. She kept the Nolte sisters' mother, *Omaatje* (little grandmother), company. Some days, Sabine snuck down to the first floor to visit the Boessenkool family, who were good friends with the Noltes. Sabine had met the family earlier, before she went into hiding, when she had come to Tante Agnes' apartment for private lessons. Sabine volunteered to help Mrs. Boessenkool with her three little sons, whom Sabine affectionately nicknamed her little *apies* (monkeys).

Tante Agnes hid an illegal radio behind some books on a bookshelf in the attic room. Evenings, she would come up and listen to news reports with Sabine. The attic had two clerestory windows. Sabine vividly remembered hearing the welcome drone of Allied airplanes on their way to bomb Germany. Through the clerestory windows, she watched searchlights penetrate the dark skies, moving around to locate the Allied planes. She heard the sounds of anti-aircraft guns and watched puffs of smoke from the guns made visible by the searchlights. She hoped and prayed that the Allied planes would not be shot down.

The next chapters cover Sabine's *onderduik tijd*, the time she went into hiding in the North Holland countryside. (*Onderduikers* is a Dutch term that translated literally means "under-divers," i.e. people who dive underground to go into hiding.) When I had nearly completed writing this part of the history, I decided to go through piles of documents Sabine had either given me or left us, just to make sure I hadn't missed anything. I had. I found an envelope marked in pen, "to be translated when we meet again." In pencil she had written, "*van Tante Agnes*" and "*brieven uit de onderduik tijd*" (letters from the time in hiding). I had not seen the envelope before, nor the very fragile letters inside. I found seven letters from Sabine to Tante Agnes, dated from November 16, 1943 to April 16, 1944, and two from Edith, all in Dutch of course. Tante Agnes must have returned the letters to Sabine after the war.

As I anticipated, Sabine was cautious about what she wrote in those letters, for she surely knew about the German occupiers intercepting and opening mail. Nevertheless, the letters add new details to what she experienced in the early months of her hiding time in North Holland. Most haunting to me is the change in tone of those letters during the six months they were written. I could not sleep the night after I read them.

20

SABINE IN NORTH HOLLAND

Hiding and Working at the Crijnsen Farm

In the fall of 1943, a man came to Tante Agnes' apartment to pick up Sabine and take her in a little coupe car to a hiding place in the North Holland countryside. The man was Klaas Snip, who was sheltering Georg and Edith on his farm.

In her first and longest letter to Tante Agnes, dated November 16, 1943, Sabine describes her trip from Agnes Nolte's apartment in Amsterdam to the North Holland countryside and her first day at her new hiding place. Sabine, who had spent nearly all her life living in large cities, narrated her journey into the Dutch countryside in minute detail, much like a tourist arriving in a foreign land. The letter reflects the enthusiasm of a 16-year-old embarking on a new adventure.

It was pitch dark the night she left Amsterdam. In the coupe, only a small overhead lamp provided minimal light, headlights were off. Once outside the city, *de maan was zo vriendelijk om een beetje te schijnen* (the moon was friendly enough to light the way a bit). The car trip was quiet, neither Sabine nor Mr. Snip had any interest in *kletsen* (chattering or talking).

The car was dropped off (why is not explained) a few miles away from Mr. Snip's farm. Mr. Snip and Sabine unloaded her suitcases onto two bicycles for the rest of the trip. Sabine had difficulty steering; she felt as if she had forgotten how to ride a bicycle during her months of recuperation from the appendectomy. "I wobbled so idiotically back and forth, that I wonder now how I could have stayed seated."

And then it began raining. While pedaling in the rain, she needed to blow her nose but could not because she didn't dare try to steer her bicycle with just one hand. "Finally, I felt pity for my poor body and asked Oom Klaas to step off the bicycle for a moment." She quickly blew her nose and then got back on the bike and continued pedaling, sometimes with the wind and sometimes against the wind, with Mr. Snip's hand extended to brace her back. "I felt like a machine that kicked, kicked and kicked some more." After what felt like hours, they arrived at Mr. Snip's house.

Tante Liesbeth en Oom Guus (code names for her parents) were very happy to see her for the first time in months. (Rather than use full names, Sabine often called people in her narratives her aunts or uncles.) Sabine was glad she had brought a good pair of shoes along because the ones she wore on the rainy bike ride were certainly "melted," she wrote. "And my asthma bothered me, but that's hardly any wonder."

Sabine exchanged gifts with her parents. From Tante Agnes, she brought a pair of slippers and half a roll of toilet paper, keeping the other half roll for herself. Her parents gave her a pair of boots and darning thread. She described it as a delightful trade. Her parents expressed unhappiness with their placement on Snip's farm. (In the early part of their hiding years, Georg and Edith still had some money left to pay for their room and board.)

Sabine stayed at the Snip's house overnight. The next day, the weather was still bad but cleared up somewhat toward the evening so Mr. Snip and Sabine could begin the bicycle ride to Sabine's new hiding place. The destination was a farmhouse in Wagenpad, in an area of land reclaimed from the sea called Wieringermeer. You can find it on the northern tip of the map of North Holland, bordering the IJsselmeer.

The moon was obscured, so they pedaled in low light. "I naturally had asthma again. *Maar nu begon het spelletje pas* (But now the game was just beginning)." Mr. Snip pedaled next to her. "Uncle Klaas had to serve as a support pillar when I was panting. I let him lead the ride. After a while my breath started to work and I could pedal myself." Mr. Snip increased the pace. "Now and then you see a farm, then all of a sudden a rabbit or a mouse, then another farm, then nothing other than the handlebars of your bike." After about an hour of hard pedaling, they arrived at the farm owned by the Crijnsen family.

The first thing Sabine noticed was a large building, "at least [large] for here, though no *wolkenkrabber* (skyscraper), and on the other side of the way, another one." She and Mr. Snip walked down a pebbled path to the house, and he pressed on an electric doorbell. When no one answered, Mr. Snip rapped on a window.

"Then just like a novel, the door was opened," she wrote to Tante Agnes. Sabine first had to take off layers of clothes she had worn for the journey. She imagined that her "foster mother" (code for Mrs. Crijnsen) must have thought initially that Sabine was fat and strong before she shed her clothing.

Sabine's letter describes the Crijnsens and their house in detail. "The boss of the house: large middle, black hair, steel blue eyes, friendly and warm face, well dressed. She, a little round woman, a little hard of hearing, appears to be a good housewife, and friendly and pitying the poor city child. She had a darling dress on, black and gray. They both come from Limburg and speak with a soft 'g.' With each other they speak a dialect that I can hardly understand." (The Dutch Sabine had learned was spoken with a hard, guttural "g.")

The Crijnsens' son, Sabine wrote, was a little boy, around four years old, an only child and "a little spoiled and whiney." She found the boy quite different from the three boys who lived in Tante Agnes' apartment building. ("I miss my little monkeys," she wrote in brackets.)

Also at the large farm were two "volunteers" (young men evading conscription for slave labor in Germany), eight cats, horses, chickens and a barn with enormous haystacks. Sabine goes on to describe all the rooms and the furniture inside the farmhouse, down to the heaters and wash basins. She observes homemade syrup, bread and butter in the kitchen. "We ate delicious cookies and drank hot chocolate."

At 10 p.m., Mr. Snip left and Sabine went up the stairs "with soft runners" to her bedroom, which she also chronicles in detail (two-person bed, with a bedspread and heavy quilt on top, nightstand, chairs, a table, chest with a big mirror, a medicine cabinet and its contents, a colored hairbrush, etc.). "More comfortable it couldn't be, don't you find?" she wrote. "You can see everything is fancy here."

Sabine promises that in her next letter to Tante Agnes she will describe "what I do all day and how I have not yet milked [a cow] and also don't have *klompen* (wooden shoes), thus I am not yet a real farm girl."

What Sabine did not include in her first letter to Tante Agnes was an unpleasant experience she had during her bicycle trip to the Crijnsen farm. After the war she disclosed that when she started wheezing with asthma, Mr. Snip "made me get off the bike several times so he could kiss me on the mouth... Of course I could not resist. My parents were hidden in his house."

The comment in her letter to Tante Agnes that "now the game was just beginning" might have been an oblique reference to that event. "He was an old man. I didn't like it, but what was I to do?" She said she had "no experience with such things," having attended all-girl Catholic schools. The "game" during the bike ride would be a prelude for what would happen at the Crijnsen farm.

Sabine's other letters to Tante Agnes during her stay with the Crijnsens are shorter and not nearly as descriptive. Six weeks later on

January 2, 1944 she wrote: "Nothing much is happening here and I am getting used to everything. If I have now become a perfect housewife, I don't know. You see everything is good for something. It's really a good housekeeping school here, you learn every day."

Three weeks later: "I am starting to get used to the work, as I get used to everything." She comments that her mirror keeps showing a person growing fatter every day, but also stronger because she is now able to bicycle on a windy day without an asthma attack.

Sabine writes about some health issues, fever and headaches, hives and ulcers (sores) that she treats herself. She writes about a new cow named Magriet that gives more and better milk than the old cow. She tells Tante Agnes that "Oom Han" (code name for Mr. Asberg) visited her, but questions whether the visit was enjoyable for Mr. Asberg because he had to bicycle for 1½ hours in rain and snow to reach her.

Sabine gives many more details about her experiences at the Crijnsen farm in a letter, written in German to her Nissen uncles in the United States and dated May 9, 1945, shortly after the end of the war. She wrote that she found the Crijnsen farm wonderful for the first week, *"dann aber began der Spass"* (but then the fun began).

"The woman had a cheap maid this way who would not run away when she did not like it. I really learned to do housework very thoroughly there, but it was nothing to be jealous about. The farmer's wife was constantly after me, and accused me of all sorts of possible and impossible things. That would not have been so bad, but her husband apparently didn't get enough satisfaction from his wife who was seven years older, and [he] wanted to try me out a little bit. When he kissed me the first time, I was more surprised than furious. The next time, I slapped his face and he was furious."

Over the next few months, her relationship with Mr. and Mrs. Crijnsen grew increasingly frayed. "During the day, he yelled at me and complained to his wife about me, and in the evening when his wife went to bed, things were different. I always had to do the sewing at night, and I couldn't change anything."

Sabine felt she could not complain about Mr. Crijnsen's molestation to Mrs. Crijnsen because the wife would not believe her. "I couldn't very well tell the wife what her beloved husband—he had married her when she was 38—was doing behind her back." Nor did she feel she could entirely thwart Mr. Crijnsen's advances. "He would keep coming up behind me and would grab and kiss me. I would tell him to stop but he didn't. I couldn't resist because he could have put me out on the street or turned me in [to the Gestapo]."

A hypochondriac, Mrs. Crijnsen often spent her days in bed. She became increasingly critical of Sabine, and found Sabine's attitude toward her and her husband as insolent. She complained that Sabine did not follow her orders or perform tasks properly. "My beloved hostess," as Sabine termed Mrs. Crijnsen in the postwar letter, frequently told Sabine that she was *Gnadenbrot Essen*, a German expression meaning receiving free food out of mercy. Mrs. Crijnsen called Sabine a pitiful beggar, an eater of crumbs, and told Sabine that she should go on her knees to thank her mistress, Mrs. Crijnsen.

Sabine, who was fluent in Dutch without a trace of a German accent, could plausibly pass for a Dutch maid. She was able to visit the farm next door, quite a walking distance away. The neighbors, the Gijsens, were a wonderful family. "It was a relief to go there." Sabine told Mrs. Gijsen what was happening to her at the Crijnsen farm. "She [Mrs. Gijsen] said she'd love to take me in but they already had a bunch of boys from Amsterdam, three or four in hiding. She was very sympathetic."

Mrs. Crijnsen contacted a parish priest to come counsel Sabine about her insolence. A priest did come to visit and, "I told him the truth," Sabine wrote. The priest told her that as a hiding place, the Crijnsen farm was an excellent spot. "He said there was nothing to do about it and to accept it. I was 16."

Sabine worked ten to 12 hours a day, keeping the farmhouse meticulously clean, plus cooking and making bread, cheese and butter. She felt she had to work hard to earn her keep. She was grateful for the company of the two young men hiding with her, a respite from the Crijnsens' continual criticism.

During her stay with the Crijnsens, Sabine became sick and could not leave her bed for several days. After she recuperated and was able to work again, the farmer's wife accused her of taking days off because of laziness. When Sabine responded, "Why don't you ask a doctor?" Mrs. Crijnsen retorted that the doctor would not want Sabine in his own house because she was such an unwelcome guest and terrible person. The next time Sabine was sick, she did not go to bed and kept working.

Sabine received some letters from her parents during this time because the same underground worker was in charge of all three Fröhlichs. She did not write to her parents about her miserable experiences with the Crijnsens because she knew that they would become terribly worried and upset about her. She also knew how difficult it might be for the Dutch underground to find her another hiding place.

By late February 1944, the supposed insolence toward Mr. Crijnsen became intolerable for Mrs. Crijnsen. She asked Oom Klaas (Uncle Klaas), the Resistance worker in charge of hiding Sabine, to take Sabine away from their farm. One evening, two Resistance workers came by car to retrieve her.

At the time of departure, Mrs. Crijnsen told Sabine that if she apologized to Mr. Crijnsen, and if she behaved properly, she would be allowed to come back on their farm. But Sabine had no desire to stay or return.

"So I went in the dark, in a car with two men, into the unknown." Sabine was relieved to leave, but worried whether the next place would be as safe as the farm. For a long time afterwards, she felt uncomfortable with any physical contact with a man, even shaking hands.

21

A SERIES OF HIDING PLACES AND MEETING COR SCHIPPER

Brief Stay at the Vleugels' in Zwaag

The Resistance workers drove some distance on a very dark night, and then stopped in front of a small house. Sabine had no idea whether they had driven east or west. Oom Klaas told her that this would be her new home for the time being.

They went inside, and she saw a young couple who "said hello in a friendly way." Then Oom Klaas and the other worker left. The couple asked Sabine if she knew where she was, and then told her she was in Zwaag. She was happy to learn that because she knew her parents were in Zwaagdijk, a neighboring village, and she thought she might be able to visit them.

Zwaag is a small town west of the IJsselmeer in the province of North Holland. Most maps of that province show the two larger cities of Hoorn and Enkuizen where the Dutch East India Company once had offices. Between these two cities is a road, along which are the small villages Zwaag, Westwoud, Hoogkarspel, Lutjebroek, Grootebroek and Bovenkarspel. Sabine spent her hidden years in several villages along this road.

Sabine's new master and mistress were the Vleugels, who had three children and were expecting a fourth. Mr. Vleugel had a bicycle repair business, and also a small store. Mrs. Vleugel was not well, and had asked Oom Klaas if he could find help for her. The Vleugels lived in a very small house, with a tiny bedroom where the whole family slept, an even smaller kitchen, and an attic. There was a bed in the attic for Sabine, in a room improvised with wood strips. A ladder connected the upstairs and downstairs levels. When a bus went by, the whole house shook.

Sabine liked the Vleugels and found them a very sweet family. She looked forward to helping them, but arrived there sick. Mrs. Vleugel sent her to bed and called in a doctor. Sabine is not sure what the doctor diagnosed, possibly the flu or diptheria.[1] She felt bad because the Vleugels now had a sick patient instead of the help they needed. After a week, Sabine recuperated and was able to assist Mrs. Vleugel.

The tone in the first postwar letter about her three and a half months on the Crijnsen farm is somewhat sarcastic and indignant. The more contemporaneous letter to Tante Agnes, however, written on March 11 about a week after she left the Crijnsen farm, has a different tone: dispirited, disillusioned and resigned to servitude.

Are you not mad at me that I was actually thrown out of my last job? I was really not at fault. I told the chaplain everything and he understood. I trusted him and could tell him everything. That was great luck during bad luck, a new friend. But my trust in the goodness in people was really a bit shocked. How much people can change. At first I thought it was heaven on earth, but how it changed. I hope never to experience something like that again. I have completely unlearned to contradict. Whatever you said, the missus was always right, as if it was also the biggest thing she told you. Rudie gave me good advice to not say anything more to her, and thus I automatically closed my mouth. That was the best. I stop now. Today is Saturday, thus still a lot of work. I've written long enough. Now to work. Thank you very much for your letter and regards to all.

Careful not to identify people by name in her wartime letters, postwar she named Kapelaan Oud as the chaplain "who rescued me from the farm in Wieringermeer." She believed the Gijsens might have informed Kapelaan Oud about her situation on the Crijnsen farm. The Rudie referred to in the March 11 letter would have been one of the boys hiding on the Crijnsen farm to evade German conscription.

In that same letter, Sabine also wrote about her relief and hope for her new hiding place. "It is very different here than there and I hope still that I can fulfill wishes here... At the moment there are many things to help with, but these are really sweet people. I do not want to leave here if they will have me."

When Sabine had not received any message from her parents for four weeks, she became worried. One morning, Mrs. Vleugel gave her a letter, delivered by a farmer from Westwoud whom the Vleugels knew. The letter was from her parents.

Georg and Edith had been moved to a new hiding place, a nice farm in the village of Westwoud (a neighboring village to Zwaag), where they lived with a farmer's widow, *Mevr. Duw Vlaar, de weduwe van Opmeer* (widow from Opmeer). Georg and Edith had spent five difficult months being confined to a small room in a house owned by Klaas Snip and his wife, a couple whom they felt had been quite mean to them and had made their lives miserable (even though the Fröhlichs had paid to stay there).

A local priest helped to find the new hiding place for the Fröhlichs. Sabine's parents were now able to go outside, had good food, and were under the care of another underground Resistance worker, Oom (Uncle) Cor Schipper, the person who had delivered the letter for Sabine to the Vleugels' home.

That evening, Oom Cor came back to the Vleugel house and asked Sabine if she would like to go to the same village where her parents were, to live with relatives of the widow. Sabine consulted with Mrs.

Vleugel, who was understanding and reluctantly let her go. "I was sorry to leave the Vleugels because I had been very happy there and didn't know where I would end up now." She worried again about what the next hiding place might be like.

Visit with the Parents

After a stay of about two and a half weeks with the Vleugels, Oom Cor came after dark and took Sabine by bicycle to the next village, Westwoud. He first brought Sabine to see her parents, who were surprised by her appearance. "They found me terribly changed because I had gotten terribly fat on the farm in Wieringermeer," Sabine remembered. "My father pronounced that I looked like a *Tonne* (barrel), with an Edam cheese on top."

Georg and Edith told Sabine that they had greatly feared for her because they had not heard from or about her in four weeks. They told her that weeks earlier, their new underground protector, Oom Cor, had informed them about a large *razzia* in Wieringemeer (where the Crijnsen farm was), and that a farmer had been arrested.

Edith and Georg did not know that Sabine had been moved. They told Oom Cor they feared that their daughter might have been arrested in that *razzia*. Oom Cor had gone to Wieringemeer with another Resistance member, Dr. Wytema, a local physician, to find out what had happened to Sabine. Her parents told her that the Resistance workers had come back to them with the good news that their Sabine was alive, healthy and living at another hiding place.

Klaas Baas' House

After the visit with her parents, Oom Cor brought Sabine to meet her new hosts, the Klaas Baas family. Mr. Baas was a stonemason with a wife and six children: three grown girls who ran the household, and three boys, the youngest of whom was Nick, aged 11. Sabine said that they received her nicely.

Nobody in the village was supposed to know that Sabine was related to the couple living with the widow. This was kept a secret in case of a betrayal or a *razzia*. Edith and Georg were known in Westwoud as evacuees from Zeeland, a coastal province that was being emptied out by the Germans. The Fröhlichs rarely spoke with anybody in town, but when they did, they explained their accent was because they came from Zeeland. That was not implausible or questioned because most people in Westwoud had probably never spoken with a real Zeeuw or heard the Zeeland dialect.

Sabine's cover story was that she was a friend of the Baas girls from the province of Gelderland. Because Sabine spoke Dutch without an accent, it was not as dangerous for her to converse with the local villagers.

The Baas daughters had just started spring-cleaning when Sabine arrived—in late-March 1944. In Holland then, spring-cleaning was an arduous, annual ritual. Everything was removed from closets and drawers for cleaning. Silverware was polished and carpets beaten and cleaned. Spring-cleaning was two weeks of total upheaval, with limited time for cooking. Sabine worked hard, cleaning alongside the Baas daughters, who were nice to her.

Every day, Sabine went to the widow's farm to pick up fresh milk, and was able to see her parents in the yard. What she remembered vividly about her stay with the Baases is that every evening after coffee, all the Baases took out their dentures and placed them in their rinsed-out coffee cups overnight, except for little Nick. In the Dutch countryside, even girls in their late teens and early twenties had false teeth.

One morning, Sabine noticed a great commotion and many cars across the street from the Baas house. The cars were in front of Dr. Wytema's home. In the middle of the previous night, three people had come to the doctor's home, rung his doorbell, and gotten him out of his bed. There had been a car accident, the men claimed, and the doctor was needed. The men shot the doctor at his front door. Dr. Wytema's pregnant wife was at the top of the stairs and heard the shot. She screamed. By the time she reached the bottom of the stairs, it was too late; her husband was dead.

Later it was learned that the perpetrators had been *landwachters* (landguards), the Dutch Nazi paramilitary organization considered traitors by the local populace. The *landwachters* shot the doctor, a known Resistance worker, in revenge for several of their own being shot during a fight with the Resistance. The *landwachters* were very dangerous for the Resistance movement because they were locals from the area. In small towns, it was often an open secret as to who worked for the underground. The terrible news that Dr. Wytema had been shot to death spread through the town and the country. His funeral became a demonstration, attended by hundreds of people from all over the Netherlands.[2]

Sabine wrote two brief letters to Tante Agnes, dated March 22 and April 16, while she was at the Baas house. In the March letter, she writes that she has now become a potato peeler, as the new family goes through a large pail of potatoes per warm meal. She plays piano, helps with the household, laughs and talks with the "very nice" girls and teases the young boys. The tone of the letter is upbeat.

In the last letter, Sabine writes she is worried about Tante Agnes because Agnes had to cancel a visit to Sabine and her parents for health reasons. Sabine asks for some articles of clothing that she left behind and gladly accepts an offer of some schoolbooks. She signs off with get well wishes from "your loving niece, Fie." (Her assumed name at the time was Sophie Fredericks, with the nickname Fietje or Fie.)

While Sabine lived with the Baas family, she had repeated outbreaks of severe hives. Dr. Bosch, a physician from a neighboring town, came several times to treat the hives. He did not think the milieu and the hard work at the Baas house were conducive to Sabine's health. He proposed that she become a nanny to his family of five children instead—his wife was expecting a sixth child. Sabine suspected the Baases wished for her to stay with them for her household help, but Dr. Bosch won. In June 1944, after about three months with the

Baases, Sabine was moved to Lutjebroek to live in the Bosch household, where it seemed to her that the doorbell rang all day long for the doctor's services.

My Parents meet

Sabine enjoyed living with and working for the family of Dr. Bosch. The Bosches were cultured people, she said, and did not treat her as just a servant or scrub lady. She appreciated conversations about topics other than local gossip about the baker and the neighbors. She was kept very busy caring for the doctor's children.

One afternoon, a handsome, tall young man rang the doorbell at the Bosch home. As was typical for the northern Dutch, he was blond haired and blue eyed. He was dressed in a trench coat and wore a felt hat. Mrs. Bosch opened the door. The man did not identify himself. He asked about the identity card for Fietje.

Sabine was terrified that the man had come to arrest her. She thought he was a Dutch police detective working for the Gestapo, and she panicked. She assumed that her parents had been arrested and now it was her turn, and that Dr. Bosch would be next. Mrs. Bosch was frightened too. Mrs. Bosch told the young man that he had better wait until her husband came home. Mrs. Bosch then told Sabine, "I am afraid they have found you," and instructed her to wait in the room next door.

Shortly afterwards, Dr. Bosch came home. He walked into the room where the young man was waiting and said, "*Goeie Dag, Meneer Schipper*" (Good Day, Mr. Schipper). Dr. Bosch knew the young man: he was Cornelis Nicolaas Schipper. His namesake uncle, Oom Cor Schipper, who had visited Sabine at the Vleugels' and moved her to the Baas home, had sent his nephew to write down the number on Sabine's false identity card to help the Resistance obtain more ration cards for her. Oom Cor had recruited his nephew into the Resistance.

And that's how my parents met. "A nice way to get acquainted, don't you think? We had been scared silly," Sabine later wrote to her uncles.

She was 17, dark haired and hazel eyed, an exotic beauty for that part of the blond world. He was 26 and became smitten.

22

THE SCHIPPER AND BUIS FAMILIES

Cornelis (Cor) Nicolaas Schipper was born at home with the help of a midwife on November 23, 1917, in the small country village of Hoogkarspel in North Holland. Cor was the third of four children, and the only son of our grandparents, Nicolaas (Klaas) Schipper and Maria Elizabeth Schipper, née Buis. My grandparents later took in a fifth child, an orphan named Lena. They raised her, but never formally adopted her.

Klaas and Maria Elizabeth could each trace their Dutch lineage back for many generations.[1] Grandfather Klaas, born April 25, 1888, was the 11th of 12 children of Cornelis (Kees) Schipper (1859-1921) and Afra Maria Schipper, née Schouten (1859–1902). Afra died with the birth of her 12th child. After her death, the children were split up and sent to live with different relatives because the father could not manage such a large family alone. According to Cor, his grandfather Kees drank a lot and the wealth in the family came from the mother's side, the Schouten clan.

Take a look at the photograph of grandfather Klaas with his 11 siblings taken in 1939 for his 25th wedding anniversary with Maria Elizabeth Buis. They are posed in front of Klaas' home in Hoogkarspel. Large families were common in the Dutch countryside.

Though separated during childhood, the 12 Schipper children remained a close-knit clan. They are significant to our story because the large Schipper clan and their children, Dad's generation, could trust each other, forming a natural network. During the German occupation, multiple family members became part of the *verzet*, the Resistance. They were all Catholic. You are looking at "Righteous Gentiles" (Non-Jews who risked their lives to save Jews during the Holocaust).

Great-grandfather Kees was a dairy farmer, but grandfather Klaas did not care for that kind of life so when he inherited a good deal of land in 1912, he decided to start growing vegetables and flower bulbs. He was among the first to grow bulbs in the northern part of the Netherlands. Previously, most of the bulb production was in the southern coastal part of the country where the soil is sandy and easier to work with. The soil in the northern part is mostly clay. Klaas exported bulbs and produce to Germany.

Later, he lost heavily because of the hyperinflation in Germany in the early 1920s. At some point during the postwar inflation, he bartered and was paid with freight cars filled with staircases and window frames. Selling these in Holland resulted in little more than recouping the cost of the rail freight that he had to pay in advance.

Despite the setbacks, Klaas stuck with growing flower bulbs and increased his acreage. According to Sabine, the Schippers were among the elite or "nobility" in the town of Hoogkarspel. (Cor, a reticent and modest man, would never say this, as it would sound boastful.) Klaas Schipper served on the board of directors of the public works (waterways and roads) of the district of Drechterland, the board of the farmers' loan bank of Hoogkarspel, and was an elder in the local Catholic church. Their three-story brick house on Streekweg, the main road in town, was one of the largest and most attractive in Hoogkarspel. A housekeeper lived with the family.

I remember my grandfather Klaas as a jolly man with an easy smile and a mischievous sense of humor. He played billiards with a group of friends every Saturday in Hoorn. In a picture of him standing with his billiard buddies, he is wearing a *boutonniere* made of miniature billiard balls. When Opa Klaas visited us in the United States in the 1970s, he brought along a whoopee cushion and used it on several of us.

Our grandmother Maria Elizabeth was one of nine children born to Jacob Simon Buis and Alida Schilder. Her grandfather, Johannes Buis (1834–1914), was the *burgemeester* (mayor) of Opdam. Her mother died young, so she had to help raise her siblings.

I remember my Oma Schipper as the more serious and stern of the two grandparents. She was kind but also a firm disciplinarian. When my grandfather made some bad investments, she helped keep the family afloat with funds she had set aside.

My Dutch Oma showed me pictures of Cor as a very young child. He had long ringlets of blond hair and wore a white dress. In those days, girls and boys were dressed alike for their first few years. Cor went to school in a neighboring town, Westwoud, for six years and then was sent to Canisius College, a boarding school in Nijmegen. He was only able to stay there for two years because it became too expensive at 1,000 guilders a year.

Opa Klaas could no longer afford the tuition because of bad loans. My cousin Marga explained the details of the family financial crisis to me. Klaas had cosigned loans for shipments of lumber for a business that failed. Back then, Marga said, people didn't declare bankruptcy to get out of debt; they worked and gradually paid off debts. And that's what Klaas did. Cor expressed no disappointment or resentment about being taken out of the boarding school because of his family's unstable finances.

After leaving the Nijmegen school, Cor traveled by bus to the town of Hoorn, a former Dutch East India Company base, for three years to attend the equivalent of middle school. At age 14 or 15, he began working after school in his father's business, peeling and cleaning flower bulbs. In 1933, at 16, he was sent to Leigh-on-Sea, England, to live with a couple, the Hayes, and learn English. This fluency in

English was intended to help the Schipper family with the flower bulb export trade.

Cor returned to England several times to book orders for flower bulbs, a difficult task during the Depression because people had little money to spare. Cor's English fluency later proved invaluable during the war for radio communications between the Dutch Resistance and British and Canadian pilots.

Asked if he ever wanted to do something other than join his father's business, Cor answered he had thought about becoming an architect. The inspiration for this idea came from a big stone Lego-type set he was given at age four or five. He loved to build houses and castles with those stones. He cut off any further questioning about becoming an architect, saying it was a brief idea and unimportant. He said he had also been interested in becoming a doctor, but not seriously so.

Cor was conscripted into the military service for six months, sometime between 1936 and 1938, and came back home after his service. We have a packet of postcards he wrote home, mostly terse complaints about being bored and bad food.

In late 1939, Cor was mobilized to the Utrecht Front and was assigned to the *loopgraven* (trenches) in the middle of the country, along the waterline of Holland. The plan was to open the dikes to inundate the land in the hope that it would halt the German army.

On May 9, 1940, when invasion looked imminent, Cor wrote a letter to his parents and sisters:

> *Dear Father, Mother and Sisters,*
>
> *I'll just write a quick note.*
>
> *What we have feared for so long has come and what will the end be? I am not afraid because my conscience is good and I face the future with confidence.*

I and all the guys have been with the Army Priest. After an Act of Repentance we have all received the General Absolution and the Papal blessing. So they can only take my life but not my soul which is with God.

I hope and am sure that you pray a lot for me and I will pray too. We are all willing to fight and die for our homeland.

I don't want to say much about the future. We are all calm. We have received the order that we must send all private possessions home. I don't have much and it's handier to keep a suitcase here.

I am going to end because I am still very busy getting ready for tomorrow. Father, Mother, Ali, Afra, Annie and Leen all the best and I thank Father and Mother for everything they have done for me. Give all family members and friends the best regards. I will pray a lot and then everything will be fine. So don't be afraid.

I'll write again as soon as possible.

Best, Cor

The Germans invaded the Netherlands the next day. When the war began, the Dutch plan was successful in flooding the land, but useless against parachutists who landed on dry land on the west side of Holland. Cor saw waves of Nazi airplanes on their way to drop parachutists in South Holland and The Hague, and to drop the bombs that destroyed Rotterdam. He shot at the Nazi airplanes with his rifle, even though he knew it was futile. One German pilot shot back with a machine gun before crashing. (Later in the war, Cor witnessed an American plane being shot down by the Germans.)

The Dutch had to surrender in five days, on May 15. The Germans interned Cor with the other Dutch soldiers in a prison camp near Utrecht. Cor described his military career as six months of training, three months of waiting and four days of fighting. He was promoted to corporal, which he did not really want because he felt nothing was different, just more responsibility. When granddaughter Laura asked him if he was proud to be fighting in the army, he replied, "No, I was not proud. But you have to do your duty."

Cor's father visited him at the prison camp and brought him flowers —to Cor's chagrin; he was hoping for cigarettes or food. Cor was released after six weeks, along with other soldiers who had "useful" trades such as agriculture to supply food. During the German occupation, Cor and his father were forced to switch crops to become vegetable growers, although they kept some land for bulbs. They grew onions, carrots, potatoes, cabbage, celery seed and carrot seed, and sold their crops at auction on the open market. The Germans bought large quantities of food through wholesalers.

Cor became involved in the Dutch underground movement in 1942 through his namesake uncle, Oom Cor Schipper. It was difficult to interview my father about his underground and Resistance work. He didn't understand why I was interested in "that old stuff." He rarely volunteered much information; I had to extract it, like pulling out teeth. If he answered questions at all, it was brief with a clear signal that I should find other topics to talk about with him. He rejected any notion that he was a hero or that what he did during the war years was heroic. He felt that what was happening in his country was wrong. He believed that the values he was raised with obligated him to oppose the immorality of the occupation and the occupiers.

When my daughter Laura asked him why he joined the underground, his answer was concise: "Because I was for the British and against the Germans." In response to written questions from Laura for a high school report about his underground work during 1944, he wrote: "It was necessary to stop Hitler, [there was] no other way. All dictatorship is bad, be it from the right or left... I admired Churchill the most with his consistency and will to fight."

He told Laura that his parents did not know he was working for the Resistance at first, and he did not discuss it with them because the less they knew, the better it was. He did not remember when his parents found out about his Resistance work, and did not think there was ever a discussion about it. "It was not something people discussed. It was safer that way."

Cor said his uncle, Oom Cor, joined the underground because of his ideals and because he did not want to be suppressed by the Germans. The younger Cor greatly admired his uncle. Oom Cor first got involved in the underground movement to help obtain food for refugees. *"Wij verzorgden voedsel voor de onderduikers,"* Cor said (We took care of food for the hidden persons).

Voedselbonnen (ration cards) were required to obtain edibles for the *onderduikers* who were mainly Jewish people and young Dutch men evading conscription work—in effect slave labor—in German factories. Oom Cor made contacts with the underground and worked with someone who stole ration cards from distribution centers.

Cor also helped his uncle to find homes for people who went into hiding. I asked how he knew whom to approach about hiding people, a very dangerous task. He answered that he knew beforehand the people he would feel comfortable asking to hide refugees. None of his close friends or relatives became Nazi sympathizers, so they were approachable. The farmhouse of his uncle Jan and Aunt Marie Schipper became a transit house for about 200 onderduikers, with stays ranging from a day to three years. Jan's sons Jaap and Hil would take the onderduikers from their father's farm to another hiding destination. Uncle Kees Schipper who lived next door to his brother Jan hid two Jewish children in his home.

Cor did meet some pro-Nazi conscripts when he was in the military service. All the Catholic priests and bishops, he said, were anti-Nazis. His local priest, Pastoor Mol, found hiding places for the Fröhlichs. Later in the war, his own parents had eight people hiding in the attic of their house.

According to Cor, the underground in North Holland initially focused on saving people, and only later engaged in sabotage against the German occupation forces. The "real" Resistance organization came into being in 1942 or 1943, he said. The Resistance derailed trains, demolished radio broadcast towers, destroyed registration lists in Amsterdam, and made contact with the British.

23

OOM COR ARRESTED, HIDDEN PERSONS RELOCATED

In June 1944, a few weeks after Cor and Sabine first met, Cor returned to the Bosch home. He brought the bad news that his uncle, Oom Cor, had been arrested. The arrest happened because two young boys in hiding (to evade forced labor in Germany) had betrayed him to the Dutch Nazis.

The boys were walking on the street—in public against the underground's rules—when a car with *landwachters* drove by. The *landwachters* were all members of the NSB (Nationaal Socialistische Beweging), the Dutch Nazi party. The boys panicked and started running. The Nazi collaborators became suspicious, and stopped them. When the NSBers questioned the boys, they gave up the name of Oom Cor Schipper as the person who hid them and obtained rations for them.

About those young boys who betrayed Oom Cor, Sabine wrote: "Why not [say] Dr. Wytema, to whom they could not do anything against anymore. Oom Cor was warned, brought his radio and his other hidden persons to a secure place, but stayed home. Of course, he was arrested..."

After his arrest, Oom Cor Schipper was brought to a police station in Hoorn. Although the Resistance members were confident that Oom Cor would not betray them, everyone understood that the Gestapo might use torture to force him to reveal the names of other Resistance workers and the *onderduikers*.

The night after Oom Cor's arrest, Cor slept in the fields, concerned his uncle might reveal his name under torture. What Cor did *not* tell us until 2017—more than seven decades later—was that he saw his uncle in Hoorn a day after the arrest, as his uncle was being led from the police station in Hoorn for transport to Amsterdam.

The Dutch police station was where the *landwachters* had their offices. "It was terrible to see because he [Oom Cor] could barely walk," Cor recounted to his son Chris in 2017.[1] The clear implication was that Oom Cor had been tortured. Chris said Dad had tears in his eyes as he recalled the scene from 70 years earlier. He was the last family member to see his uncle alive.

From Amsterdam, Oom Cor was sent to the Dutch concentration camp in Vught. A medical dossier on Oom Cor, stored at the National Institute of War Documentation, noted he was already ill when he was transferred to that camp. The Germans dismantled camp Vught in September 1944 and sent the male prisoners, including Oom Cor, to the Sachsenhausen concentration camp in Oranienburg near Berlin, Germany. He perished there on October 31, 1944, aged 45.

The younger Cor returned home after spending a night in the fields and seeing his uncle being led out of the police station in Hoorn. Cor had a deep disdain for the NSBers, calling them the real criminals in the war, worse than the Germans.

A ditty of the times about the Dutch Nazis went:

> *Op de hoek van de straat staat een NSB'er,*
> *'t is geen mens, 't is geen dier,*
> *'t is een farizeeer.*
> *Met de krant in de hand,*

staat hij daar te venten.
En verkoopt zijn Vaderland,
voor slechts enk'le centen.

(On the corner stands an NSBer,
it's not a person, it's not an animal,
it's a Pharisee.
With the newspaper in hand,
he stands there peddling.
And sells his Fatherland
for just a few cents.)

The reality was that many more Dutch were collaborators with the Nazis than took part in the Resistance; the majority just tried to get by and remained uninvolved. Cor expressed annoyance at people who joined the Resistance in the last month or two of the war, then took credit as heroes in postwar parades. "Where were they in the beginning when they were needed?" he asked.

Relocating Hidden Families after Oom Cor's Arrest

Cor now had to quickly relocate all the persons hidden under Oom Cor's protection. In all, he had to move 35 families and create new papers for them. The local priest, Pastoor Mol, assisted in finding new homes.

One of the families needing relocation after Oom Cor's arrest was Georg and Edith Fröhlich. By mid-1944, Georg and Edith had been out of Germany for five years and were running out of money, so they could not contribute toward household expenses as they had in previous hiding places.

"I slept with your parents before I slept with you," my father volunteered out of the blue while I was interviewing Mom about her war years during a visit to Medford Leas, N.J. in 2011. My mother looked up, surprised; she had not heard that story before. My father explained, "I had to take them away to a new hiding place. I slept with your parents on a haystack in the fields of Westwoud." He had to spend that night outside with the elder Fröhlichs before he could move them to a new safer location.

Cor initially moved the Fröhlich parents from the widow's farm in Westwoud to the farm of Mr. Rentenier in Hoogkarspel. Mr. Rentenier was a reticent bachelor who had a housekeeper with a reputation as village gossip. She became afraid, constantly imagining *landwachters* were surveying or approaching the farmhouse in search of hidden persons. Cor became concerned the Rentenier farm was not a safe hiding place with the edgy housekeeper, so he moved Georg and Edith Fröhlich to the home of his oldest sister, Alida (Ali) Buijsman, in the town of Grootebroek.

Ali had three young children and was in her ninth month of pregnancy with a fourth. A midwife would need to be called soon to Ali's home, so the Fröhlichs could not stay there long. My Tante Ali vividly recalled when Georg first entered the house. He was an imposing presence, a dignified, tall and serious man, with pince-nez glasses. Georg always kept his back to windows, Ali told me. Wanting to feel useful, he peeled potatoes with her. He asked Ali to save for him any papers with words on them, telling her, "If you don't read, your brain rusts." The Fröhlichs left after a few days for a hiding place in another town, Bovenkarspel.

Cor and his father introduced Georg and Edith to Jan Elders, the mayor of Bovenkarspel. The mayor promised to find a hiding place for the Fröhlichs, but ended up taking them by car to live in a room in his own home. Mr. Elders gave the Fröhlichs new false identification papers, renaming them Gerard and Elizabeth Faessen, and registered them as evacuees from Limburg, a province in the south of the Netherlands where residents speak with a Limburg dialect.

The Elders had eight children. Georg Fröhlich dubbed the Elders home as *"Huize Elastiek,"* the Elastic House. Georg and Willy (Wilhelmina) Elders, one of Mayor Elders' daughters, kept a diary of daily life at Huize Elastiek during the last year of the German occupation. Willy's eldest son, Leo Wiegman, translated and published the diary in 2017.[2]

After Oom Cor's arrest, Sabine was moved from Dr. Bosch's home to the home of a school principal, Meester van der Vlugt, and his eight children in Westwoud. The principal was active in the Resistance; his wife managed a household of 12 that included two boys evading German conscription. Sabine remembered Mrs. Vlugt as a beautiful woman. Sabine stayed there only five days because it became unsafe; the young curious van der Vlugt children could not keep a secret and told too many people in town about their "interesting visitor."

Despite the short stay, Sabine made a strong impression on one of the children, Trudy, who was eight or nine at the time and later became a lifelong friend. Trudy recalled that she first saw Sabine, then named Fietje Fredericks, at church with the Baas family who sat in the second row of pews in front of the third row used by the van der Vlugt family. (In small Dutch towns, locals tend to quickly notice the presence of non-locals.) When she appeared as a guest at their home for a short time, Trudy did not know that Fietje was an *onderduiker*.

Fietje read to the children at night before they went to sleep. When some people asked her if the couple that lived with Duw were her parents, she responded by laughing and saying she didn't even know those people. "That must have been horrible for her," Trudy wrote me in an email sharing her memories. Such curiosity underscores the danger of hiding in a small town where everyone knows everyone else and where the presence of outsiders attracts attention.

Like others, Trudy remembered that Sabine spoke Dutch fluently without an accent so passed as Dutch. "I was younger at the time and I adored her, but our family with many children was too dangerous for her."

Because the van der Vlugt home was deemed too risky, Pastoor Mol then approached another family, the Schapers in the neighboring town of Hoogkarspel, about taking in a child in hiding.

24

THE SCHAPER FAMILY: "MY MOST PLEASANT HIDING PLACE"

When informed that Sabine was the daughter of a *Kantonrechter* (district court judge), Mrs. Schaper was initially hesitant to take in *het deftige meitje* (dialect for the fancy girl), concerned that she would be too formal and spoiled. When Mrs. Schaper met Sabine, however, she decided that she was a *lief kind* (sweet child) and took her in. Sabine described her next three months with the Schapers as her most pleasant hiding place.

Mr. Evert Schaper, a tall and thin man, was a carpenter. His wife (called "Stijntje") was a shorter woman who wore wire rimmed glasses and ran a small grocery store located in the front of their home. The Schapers had six children, two girls and four boys aged 11 to 23. The Schapers also had a nephew who had lived with them for six years since his mother's death. The Schaper parents slept in a bed built into an alcove, and the children slept in the attic.

The Schapers treated Sabine like a daughter. She was given a little room off the living room, with a single bed, wash basin and pitcher. It was a room that had been kept for their oldest son, Dirk, who lived in an institution for the mentally disabled but came home for occasional visits. Having a private room with a washbowl was a luxury in the Schaper home. The rest of the family shared a sink in the kitchen.

Sabine could not go outside alone safely during daylight hours, as she could when she'd hidden on a farm, because the Schapers lived in town and neighboring homes were close by. She could not let herself be seen by anyone outside of the Schaper family. When the bell rang as someone entered the Schapers' grocery store, she would hide in a curtained-off part of the house.

Jan, one of the Schaper children, wrote to Sabine in 2002 about some of his memories of Sabine's time in hiding with his family. He remembered her name at the time was Fietje Fredericks. Jan was assigned to be on watch whenever Sabine went outside in good weather to enjoy a little sun. She would walk between her room and the *schuur* (outbuilding or barn) behind the house. Jan wrote: "I had to sit under the pear tree with a view of the street so if anyone came along the path near our windows, I had to cough so you would have time to quickly go inside. Evenings when it was dark you went outside once with mother to get some fresh air and took a little walk along the fruit trees and through the vegetable garden."

Father Schaper used his vacation time in the summer of 1944 to build a space in the attic with a screen, where Sabine could sit in the fresh air and the sun without being seen by neighbors. When it was dark at night, she walked around in the little back yard. Sabine felt it was a miracle that none of the neighbors discovered her.

In the Dutch countryside, neighbors and visitors come to the back door, so it was customary to always keep the back door open for visitors to knock on and enter. When Sabine was hiding at their home, the Schapers kept their back door closed all the time— something that could easily raise suspicion.

The Schapers therefore came up with an explanation for their locked back door—Piet Rood. Piet was a junk man who lived near their house and was "not quite right in the head." As Sabine described him, "He was just off his rocker. He was harmless." His reputation was that he never washed himself, ate slugs and dead cats, and wore women's stockings and knee pants. For 25 cents, Piet would walk around in his underwear down the street—to the amusement of the whole village. Piet Rood was well known in the area, from Hoorn to Enkhuizen. One of Piet's odd habits was to make unannounced and unwanted visits to local homes. Thus the Schapers explained to neighbors that their locked back door was a defense against Piet's visits.

When a neighbor came and rapped on their back door, the Schapers went very slowly to open it, giving Sabine enough time to vanish into her little room next to the living room. She spent hours, and sometimes days, in that little room.

Despite these confining circumstances, Sabine had a wonderful time at the Schapers' home. She would play games and have fun with the children. Pastoor Mol provided her with some books. She helped with washing dishes and sewing, but did little housework compared with her previous hiding places. They spoiled her.

She was able to listen to a radio, with broadcasts of Dutch and German news. The news reports from the German army were of particular interest to her. She meticulously marked her map to track the German army's retreats, called *Planmäsig geräumt* meaning cleared according to plan, the euphemistic term the Germans used for withdrawals, in France and then in Belgium.

Cor Schipper came to visit Sabine at the Schapers' two or three times, carrying letters from her parents, and gifts of food—grapes and butter, luxury items in those times. The Schapers teased Sabine about the visitor and his gifts. The food was very welcome because that was becoming scarce. The Schaper family had two goats, and went gleaning, picking leftovers from a wheat harvest for a week so that they could bake bread.

When Sabine became sick, the Schapers took wonderful care of her. Dr. Bosch would come to treat her when necessary for her asthma and illnesses. Once he was called to see Sabine for a badly cut right hand. Sabine as Fietje wrote about that cut hand, as well as a bout of flu in letters to her Oom and Tante (code for her parents) in August and September 1944. Mrs. Schaper added a note to one letter, telling the Fröhlichs not to worry about Sabine's healing hand and reassuring them that she calls a doctor in whenever their daughter is not well. Mrs. Schaper writes that she has no regret about taking in their daughter in, that she is helpful and that they get along well.

Sabine, in turn, in a later letter writes about how much she likes the living with the Schapers and wants very much to stay there, the longer, the better. She drew a picture of her room at the Schapers' home so her parents could visualize it, describing the room as cozy and nicely lit. Sabine writes that she studies for a while everyday, but acknowledges she has forgotten a lot. "Except for my school books, I spend almost all my day with my nose in my atlas which is decorated with an enormous number of stripes and arrows. I believe geography will become my best subject."

Sabine worries about Oom Cor: "I don't hear anything from Oom Cor at all," she writes. "How awful for his wife. We hope to see him healthy and well again." In another letter, she chides her father, now 60, for writing about growing old and joking about having one leg in the grave, commenting she does not find this funny. In the last letter I found from her Schaper days, she scolds her parents: "Put worries out of your head otherwise you will never hear my health bulletins again."

The Schapers' neighbor became very curious as to why the doctor was visiting a seemingly healthy family. Mrs. Schaper, who probably never told a lie in her life, learned to lie cheerfully and believably.

During Sabine's stay, the Schapers' daughter, Tina, developed scarlet fever. Mrs. Schaper sent Tina to the hospital rather than caring for Tina at home because she was afraid that Tina would endanger Sabine, an asthmatic prone to illnesses. Sabine found the Schapers "a wonderful family, hardworking, full of laughter and full of grace." She described this family as incredible for their kindnesses toward her.

25

CRAZY TUESDAY, COR SCHIPPER
GOES INTO HIDING

In September 1944, the Allies invaded the south of Holland. The Dutch went "crazy" ("*dol*") on Tuesday, September 5, expecting the Allies to conquer North Holland the next day. The craziness began with a false report from London that the town of Breda had fallen. From there, the stories and rumors escalated at a frantic pace: the Allies are in The Hague, in Rotterdam, in Utrecht, in Amsterdam. Tonight they will be in Alkmaar. The Germans are fleeing. The NSBers are running away. It was complete confusion: *Dolle Dinsdag* (Crazy [or Mad] Tuesday).

Cor came to the Schapers and announced that Sabine could now go out safely in public. He had news from Resistance headquarters that the Allies would be in Alkmaar, the nearest large city, by the evening. Sabine did not yet dare to go out in public; she wanted to wait until the *Tommies* (British soldiers) came. Mrs. Schaper told Sabine that Pastoor Mol had brought her into their house, and only when the pastor gave permission could Sabine go out in public. So Sabine stayed inside.

As part of the craziness on Dolle Dinsdag, Cor went to the German Nazi office in Hoogkarspel, and told the Nazis that the war was over, and that the Americans were coming the next day. He instructed the

Nazis to turn over their weapons to him because the Resistance would be taking over and he would be in charge. He was 26 then, and described this act as the most stupid thing he ever did.

Cor told the Germans they would not be harmed and could leave as long as they surrendered the headquarters and left behind their weapons. The Germans asked for 24 hours to think about it, and Cor agreed to that. When the Germans called their superiors, they were told the situation was changing on the front and not to do anything. They did not turn over their weapons and the Allies did not come the next day. The Allies were not able to cross the Rhine River into North Holland for nearly nine months. This failed Allied military operation to break through the German lines at Arnhem is known as "Operation Market Garden," the basis for the book *A Bridge Too Far* by Cornelius Ryan and a movie with the same title.

Cor's parents knew he was going to the local German headquarters to demand the Germans surrender their weapons. His parents and sisters vacated the house, knowing what he had done and fearing the NSBers would come to arrest the whole family.

Now Cor himself had to plan to go into hiding, having exposed himself as a member of the Resistance and facing certain arrest. He stayed alone in his house for two days, until the "Green Police" came to the door. He slipped out a side door of the home's sun room, and stayed outdoors, sleeping in the fields for several days. He then hid briefly in two villages in North Holland on the IJsselmeer, first at the home of an uncle (Oom Piet Schipper in Wervershoof) and then with a friend in Andijk. Lastly, he went to live at an aunt's house in Zomerdijk, part of Spanbroek in North Holland, where he stayed until the end of the war.

He sent a message to the Schapers that he had to go into hiding. He wrote Sabine a letter that he was just as locked up as she was, and that he would not be able to stand it very long. Their courtship continued by letter.

Cor's aunt, Gre Schipper, in Zomerdijk already had two male relatives as boarders and was also hiding a Jewish family of four in her attic. The Jewish family, parents and two sons, kept to themselves. The aunt brought them food upstairs. Eventually, the Jewish family had to be moved to a house in the next town because it was no longer safe in Zomerdijk; the British were dropping weapons by parachute in the area for the Resistance. The family was angry that they had to leave, but did so and survived the war.

Although Cor had to remain in hiding until liberation day, May 5, 1945, he continued his work with the Dutch Resistance. He had a radio hidden in his aunt's hayloft. He listened to the BBC and other stations for any military news, then typed it up and ran the copy through a stencil machine to make an underground newsletter, which he distributed by bicycle, giving copies to other members of the Resistance. Women also helped distribute the illegal news because they aroused less suspicion than young men, who were supposed to be working in Germany. The head of the underground newsletter, "Free Orange" (orange is the color of the Dutch royalty) was the head of the local school.

In answer to granddaughter Laura's questions about his Resistance work in 1944, Cor wrote, "Although the German occupation was getting harsher for the general population, we were getting more optimistic and daring."

26

COR'S WORK WITH THE MANDRILL RESISTANCE CELL

Cor was one of about 20 members of the "Mandrill" Resistance cell in the Zomerdijk area of the town of Spanbroek in North Holland. The headquarters for the Mandrill cell was a farmhouse belonging to his uncle, Jan Schipper. His cousin, Hil Schipper, who had studied to become a priest before the war, was the cell's leader or CAT —*Commandant Afwerp Terreinen* (Commander of Drop-Off Areas). He'd helped create a network of Resistance cells, often relying on contacts with his many Schipper relatives. Another cousin, Piet Schipper, also belonged to the Mandrill cell. Cor was the group's radio man. His code name was "Cor Klaassen."

Because Cor spoke English, he was able to use an instrument called an "S-phone," similar to a walkie-talkie, to help direct drops of weapons and other supplies from British and Canadian planes. In a newspaper article written after the war, Cor described and demonstrated how he used the S-phone to communicate with the Allied pilots. Cor also guided English parachutists into Holland. He made contacts with the British through secret agents who were dropped behind the German lines in Holland. The Resistance gave the British agents official-looking Dutch identification papers and sheltered the agents. Dutch people also trained in Britain to become British agents.

Cor said many agents were caught and killed by the Germans because of *verraders*, Dutch traitors coerced by Nazis into giving away the secret codes used to communicate with the agents. The Nazis knew when and where the agents would be dropped and were waiting for them. This was known as the *Englandspiel* (England Game), a German counterintelligence operation.

Although the Germans tried to confiscate them, the Resistance had hidden radios that received broadcasts from Radio Oranje, the Dutch liberation radio station in London. Radio Oranje would broadcast at noon and in the evening. The broadcasts included information given to Resistance cells in code about where to expect the next parachute drops. The designated fields for drops had certain code names. For instance, the code for a drop at Zomerdijk that the Mandrill Resistance cell was assigned to cover was: *"Mijn broer is ziek"* (My brother is sick). If this phrase was repeated in the noon and evening broadcasts, it meant a drop would take place at Zomerdijk.

The hope behind all the supply drops was that an armed Resistance would help the Allies liberate the country. Allied pilots dropped canisters filled with guns, but occasionally added cigarettes and chocolate, extras Cor said he really enjoyed. Resistance members gathered the canisters from the fields. Some drops landed in the canals and had to be hauled out of the water. Other times when parachutes did not open up, the canisters burrowed three feet deep into the land and had to be dug out.

Hil Schipper began a memoir about his work for the Dutch Resistance but died before he could complete it. The unpublished memoir is a fascinating read about the difficulties the various Resistance cells encountered in hiding the dropped canisters and then transporting weapons and other supplies to Amsterdam, Alkmaar and other cities.

The Mandrill members unpacked the canisters inside the farmhouse and hid the supplies under floors and haystacks. They buried the parachutes and disposed of the empty canisters, usually by dumping them in canals. Using regular trucks to distribute weapons became too dangerous after Nazis had intercepted one truck with weapons and executed the members of that Resistance cell, so Cor and the other local Resistance workers used hay wagons, milk trucks, small boats or baby carriages for distribution instead, hiding the dropped weapons under potatoes or hay during transport.

The Mandrill territory was considered the most important drop field of eight in the area of North Holland known as West Friesland. Between the first drop the night of September 8–9, 1944 and the last on April 28, 1945, the Mandrill unit received 21 codes from British intelligence about drops. In at least 12 of the 21 cases, after the announcement in code in the Dutch-language broadcast of the BBC, a weapons shipment actually followed.

Two teams were ready when the Allied plane came over, flying low, for first drop at the Mandrill field the night of September 8–9. One team shone its lights and the pilots answered back with their tail lights, turned and dropped 17 containers, including three parcels with radio transmitters and batteries. They also dropped two paratroopers, secret agents of the exiled Dutch government. One container fell somewhat slower, as it was apparently lighter. When the containers were opened, the lightest was filled with a welcome surprise: tobacco, food and snacks.

These agents were dropped only two days after the Nazis executed 40 Dutch and seven British agents in Mauthausen, victims of the German counterintelligence operation. The agents murdered in Mauthausen had been parachuted into occupied Netherlands in 1942 and 1943. Fortunately, there was no intelligence compromise for the drops at Zomerdijk; the Mandrill unit survived the war. Not so fortunate were two Dutch agents who parachuted from planes on October 7, 1944 at Dokkum, a town in Friesland about one and a half hours from Spanbroek. Germans arrested the two agents immediately after they landed.

Of the 154 tons of weapons, incendiary bombs, explosives and landmines dropped, the Mandrill unit took care of 65 tons. The Resistance units named Oliver and Sally in other nearby farmlands took three and eight drops respectively, totaling 74 tons. The unit Laloe took two drops of 15 tons. The tonnage does not take into account the quantity of food stuffs, tobacco products, refreshments and technical equipment parachuted onto the fields.[1]

Cor's most awful Memory of WWII

Not until he was 99 did Cor reveal to his son Chris his worst memory of the war: Cor was at a meeting with other members of the Mandrill group when two young German soldiers came by. It was a few months before the end of the war and the German soldiers might just have been looking for food. The clandestine meeting was, of course, illegal and the group knew what would happen if the soldiers left and informed their superiors. The Mandrill cell also had weapons stored in the house from the weapon drops. To survive themselves, they had to kill the two soldiers and hide their bodies.

Cor said one of the soldiers pleaded that he had a wife and children. Cor witnessed the killing of the two soldiers and described it as "the most awful thing I ever saw." Fearing retribution, the whole Mandrill group went into hiding for weeks.

Cor revealed this after Chris showed him a documentary about Dutch Resistance groups, including the Mandrill group.[2] Cor's cousins, Hil and Piet Schipper, were interviewed for the documentary, and Hil described the event with the two German soldiers. It helped me understand why my father did not like to tell wartime stories. Not only was he naturally modest and reticent, but some memories were very painful to recall even 70-plus years later.

I gained additional appreciation for how very dangerous the Resistance work was, especially the night-time weapon drops, when I visited the Netherlands in 2014. My cousin, Klaas Buijsman, a history buff, took my husband and me on a tour of the homes where Sabine and her parents were hidden and to sites of the Resistance cells, including the farmhouse that was the headquarters of the Mandrill group. A Schipper relative from a later generation who married into the family was still living there at the time.

The Mandrill farmhouse is a square, brick structure, with a high pitched, thatched roof and a long, attached barn in the back—very typical of that area. The house is surrounded by large, open farm fields. Cows grazed on the land next door. So pretty and peaceful now. Zomerdijk had no large water tower, church tower or other visible high structure from which the German occupiers could have overlooked the farm fields. That made it a choice area for the drops.

Nevertheless, it was extremely dangerous during the German occupation to be outside after dark, which is when all the drops occurred. Klaas told us that the Nazi occupiers would shoot on sight anyone found outside after the 8 p.m. curfew. On the other hand, the communists in the Resistance would also shoot anyone after dark, assuming the person had to be a Nazi occupier. In our travels, we passed by a road with a median strip containing a granite crucifix surrounded by geraniums and a small square of low bushes. The crucifix read: "Here fell Nico Broers on 21–2–'45, 23 years old." Nazis had executed the young man there.

On our tour, we also visited a memorial to the "Sally" Resistance group. The small memorial is on the site where the farmhouse that was the group's headquarters once stood. The memorial reads: "*waar de wolken wapens regenden*" (where the clouds rained weapons). There's a group photograph of about 22 Sally members, all so young, looking barely out of their teens. The Sally group, including two women, pose in front of the farmhouse, itself bedecked with parachutes after liberation day. The memorial has three small bronze statutes on top: a light box (to signal planes), a chicken with her beak clipped shut (to keep fowl silent during the commotion of the drops) and a model of the former farmhouse. We also saw the homes of the Oliver group (now riding stables) and the Laloe group.

27

SABINE'S LAST HIDING PLACE, THE "ELASTIC HOUSE"

Early one Sunday morning in October 1944, Wilhelmina (Will or Willy) Elders, a daughter of Mayor Jan Elders of Bovenkarspel, came by bicycle to the Schaper house, bringing news from Sabine's parents who were living in the mayor's house.

Willy extended an invitation to Sabine to attend church services in Bovenkarspel and to visit with her parents afterwards. Willy had ridden her bike while wheeling another beside her that Sabine could ride back to the Elders' home. Willy had Sabine test ride the bike to make sure she could make the trek safely to Bovenkarspel, several villages away. Sabine passed the test.

By the time the girls arrived at the Elders' home in Bovenkarspel, however, Sabine had developed a high fever. Discovering this, Georg and Edith wanted their daughter to stay with them, at least until she was better. The Elders consented, and the Elastic House stretched again to add yet another boarder.

After Sabine's arrival, Huize Elastiek held 16 people: the Elders, their maid, eight children, two nieces from Amsterdam, and the three Faessens, the new false last names for the Fröhlichs. Mayor Elders had a false ID created for Sabine, keeping the prior false first name of

Sophie (Fietje) and changing her last name to Faessen to match her parents' new false names.

Sabine remained at the Elders' home until the end of the war, sharing a room with her parents. She slept in a twin bed with her mother, so she had to learn to sleep in a scrunched-up position. Sabine said that compressing her body into a small space became a life-long sleeping habit.

Sabine and Cor stayed in contact while both were in hiding. We have a charming letter dated October 16, 1944 from Sabine to Cor, which she opens with a pretend telephone call:

Hello, hello, Fietje speaking here. Is Cor there? That's good. I'm just calling you to thank you for your warm visit-letter. How are you doing? With me things are splendid.

Sabine relates how she went to visit her parents, became sick and ended up staying with the Elders family. She explains she could not "call" Cor earlier because just that day she had met Cor's parents who gave her Cor's address. She continued,

How much your father looks like Oom Cor, say. I think of him often, how would he be doing? How is your health? Is it going all right? Are you still bored or bothered by the cold? So many questions, but maybe I will get answers.

At the time she wrote the letter, the Schippers had not yet learned Oom Cor's fate.

Sabine wrote about what the Elder boys were studying and described how she played piano with an Elders "orchestra" consisting of a flute, an imitation saxophone, two baritones and one soprano.

We laughed so hard. On the other hand, it felt strange to be so cheerful when a few kilometers away [there is] so much sadness and suffering. I believe it probably is a reaction to the awful and tragic things that we hear about. Whenever will the end come?

Sabine closed the letter by sending regards from her family and her best wishes for his wellbeing.

The final winter of the war, the Fröhlichs did not have to stay hidden in the Elders' house all the time. Jan Elders told villagers that a former colleague and his wife were visiting him from Limburg when the Allies invaded the south of Holland. The Faessens obviously could not return home to Limburg because the south of Holland had been cut off from rest of the country. Mayor Elders also told people that residents of Limburg spoke Dutch the way the Faessens did, to explain Georg and Edith's heavy accents.

In late November 1944, the Nazi police told Jan Elders that he had to confiscate all bicycles from Bovenkarspel residents for German use. The Resistance movement opposed the confiscation. Mayor Elders knew that if he did not carry out the Nazi orders, he would be arrested. So the mayor and all the occupants of his home had to go into hiding at once.

The Elders children were farmed out to their grandparents, the local doctor, friends and local relatives. Dad's sister Ali graciously agreed to accept the three Faessens at her home in Grootebroek. In the dark, the Elders, with the help of a few neighbors, emptied their house of all their belongings. The Faessens transported their few belongings at night by bicycle to Grootebroek.

The next morning, Resistance members met at their headquarters and decided it would be better to have the mayor stay in his post. With great relief, residents returned to the bare Elastic House. Because the curtains had been removed, people in town noticed the emptiness in the mayor's home. They began to ask if the mayor had been forced to go into hiding. The townspeople were told that the furniture had been moved for a big house cleaning. For credibility, the Huize Elastiek's residents did indeed clean the house from top to bottom to a shine. Then slowly, from back roads and over canals, the furnishings were returned to Huize Elastiek.

The first piece of furniture that came back and was put in immediate use was the radio, the most important, treasured and used piece of furniture. As mayor and civilian head of police services, Jan Elders was permitted to keep his radio, but forbidden to listen to broadcasts from England. Of course, he ignored this ban. Good friends of the Elders, including the local pastor, postmaster and doctor, regularly dropped by to visit Mayor Elders, coincidentally arriving at the beginning of BBC and Radio Oranje broadcasts, and departing once they'd ended.

"Honger Winter"

Next came the *Honger Winter* (Hunger Winter). With South Holland cut off, there was a severe food shortage, especially in the cities of North Holland. When possible, parents in cities sent their children to live with relatives and friends in the countryside to avoid starvation. Later in the winter, many starving city dwellers left the cities and trekked through the countryside in search of food.

People from Amsterdam would knock on my Dutch grandmother's door and offer silverware in exchange for a potato. My grandmother told me about one person who hid in her attic and stayed in bed most of the time so as to use minimal energy and require minimal food during that Hunger Winter. She also spoke of a young German soldier who came to her house and showed her pictures of his family. I was so impressed by her compassion; she viewed this soldier as a fellow human, a young, homesick boy, and not solely as the German enemy.

One family gave Jan Elders a piano in exchange for a supply of potatoes. Sabine was the only person at the Elders house who could play the piano, and she did. Years later, one of the Elders' sons, Wim Elders, told Sabine that listening to her play piano was the beginning of his interest in music. He became a music professor in Utrecht. Another Elders son, Jaap, said that his discussions with Georg about law and history influenced him to become a lawyer.

Sabine recalled with a smile how people read cookbooks for entertainment. When a recipe called for a dozen eggs or so, it was considered hilarious, and people laughed at the impossibility of assembling such ingredients. The Germans confiscated food and sent food supplies in trains to Germany with large letters on boxcars proclaiming, "From the Grateful People of the Netherlands."

During the Hunger Winter, a friend of the Elders family, a university professor in Amsterdam, asked Jan Elders to find a country home for his daughter because of the food shortages in the city. The daughter, Netty van der Donk, was placed with a family in Bovenkarspel. Netty was a school friend of Sabine from her days at the Reynier-Vinkeleskade School. Jaap Elders, the oldest son of the Elders, gave Sabine and Netty private lessons in Latin, physics and other subjects. Jaap had begun university studies before the war and used his university texts to tutor the girls.

The Hunger Winter also brought fuel shortages. People cut trees to burn for warmth, and the cities were virtually denuded. Electricity also became scarce. When there was current on the wires, the Elders would quickly try to make use of electric cooking before the current stopped. Cooking a warm meal for 16 people twice a day on a wood stove was a challenge.

Meals depended on the wind and other available energy sources. On the roof, the Elders constructed a gadget to produce electricity by harnessing the wind. What little electricity could be stored went to the radio. When there was no electricity or gas, people constructed and used *wonderkachels* (wonder stoves). These stoves were a tubular contraption capped with a single burner. People would tear up telephone books and feed the paper into the bottom of the tube to create kindling for the burner on top.

For light, the Elders used kerosene lamps, which smelled bad, exploded periodically, and gave little light. Of the 16 people at the Elders' home, few stayed up past 7:30 p.m.; there simply was not enough light to see or do anything. On occasion, the Elders built primitive little oil lamps. These lamps were constructed using a glass of water, a cork slathered with a layer of oil or hair pomade, a razor blade and a wick connected to the cork with pins. The contraptions did not give much light, but at least people did not have to sit in the dark every night.

During the last weeks of the war, Sabine remembers the water supply was turned off. Some lucky people had water saved in barrels. Others had to wait for rain to fill pails and barrels. For laundry, cleaning toilets, etc., people used unhygienic, algae-laden canal water.

German Soldiers visit Huize Elastiek

When the Allies moved forward in the East, German soldiers came into the North Holland area around the IJsselmeer (formerly Zuider Zee). On April 16, 1945, two *Moffen* (derogatory Dutch term for Germans) came to the back of the Elders' house. The Elders' first reaction was to make the boys in hiding from conscription for forced labor disappear. Their second thought was to hide the forbidden bicycles. But the bicycles were all standing in a row behind the house, so there was no time to move them. Edith went to her bed, hiding contraband articles under the covers. Georg stayed in the attic room, where he normally spent most of his days teaching himself Spanish and English.

What did the soldiers want? Willy didn't understand German and Sabine, of course, had to pretend that she couldn't understand German either. Eventually, the soldiers communicated to the family that they wanted some milk and food. The Germans had potatoes, onions and lard with them, and wanted to fry the food themselves. The Elders let the soldiers into their kitchen.

When Sabine started to chop wood for lighting the stove, one of the soldiers decided that she was not doing the task well or fast enough. "*Fräulein, dass machen Sie nicht richtig* (Miss, you are not doing it right)," the soldier told her. The soldier took the axe and chopped the wood himself. Whenever a soldier said something to her, Sabine gestured that she was having a hard time understanding him. She could not let on that she understood German. The entire scene was surreal for her.

The German soldiers cooked and ate their meal. As they departed, the soldiers shook hands with Sabine and others. The soldiers said, "*Auf wiedersehen,*" but Sabine did not respond in kind. She washed her hands immediately after their departure.

Liberation

On May 4, 1945, Jan Elders told the Fröhlichs, "Listen... That is the [sound of the] last German truck leaving." The war had ended.

A day or two later, Sabine and her friend Netty rode bicycles all the way to Amsterdam (about 35 miles/56 kilometers) for a huge victory celebration. The trip was not smooth or easy because the bicycles had airless tires made from pieces of cut-up auto tires. On the way to Amsterdam, Sabine and Netty saw German soldiers sitting on the side of the road. They had been stripped of their weapons and were not yet able to obtain transportation home. The girls could not help smiling and feeling pleased at the sight. The girls had bicycles, forbidden to the Dutch only days earlier, while the German soldiers were stranded.

When Sabine arrived in Amsterdam, she first went to visit Agnes Nolte at her apartment. Afterwards, she joined her former classmates from the Reynier-Vinkeleskade School for the victory celebration march. Sabine was given the honor of carrying the flag for her school, and later remembered the joy and euphoria she felt during the victory celebration. But she also remembered almost fainting under the weight of the flag during the march because she had not eaten that day.

POSTSCRIPT

Thanks to Cor and other brave Dutch persons, Sabine and her parents survived the war. They were fortunate to be able to go into hiding in the Dutch countryside. The statistics posted in the Amsterdam Resistance Museum are grim:

Of the 140,000 Jews in the Netherlands at the beginning of WWII, 107,000 were deported to concentration camps where 101,500 perished and 5,500 survived.

Of the 25,000 who went into hiding, 18,000 survived, 7,000 perished.

8,000 are listed as "other" ("sterilized or otherwise").

POST-POSTSCRIPT

Part I of the family history describes research about Sabine's Jewish ancestors. A future part of the family history will cover the early postwar years. The Fröhlichs emerged from the war broke and stateless, needing to re-establish their identities and rebuild their lives. This history will include the courtship and marriage of Cor and Sabine and their emigration to the United States; Georg and Edith returning to Germany where he helped rebuild the German legal system and became a supreme court judge; Cor building a flower bulb import business, Sabine becoming an activist, and the arrival of our generation, five children. Agnes Nolte became a member of the Dutch parliament and my godmother.

NOTES

2. Searching for her Brother's Name

1. In 1999, the name RIOD was changed to NIOD, National Institute for War Documentation. In 2010, NIOD merged with the Centre for Holocaust and Genocide Studies (CHGS) to become the NIOD Institute for War, Holocaust and Genocide Studies. (www.niod.nl/en/)
2. raumdernamen.mauthausen-memorial.org
3. Herzberg, Abel J, *Kroniek der Joden-vervolging, 1940–1945* (Querido, Amsterdam 1950, 1985 ed.) pp. 125-127; Presser, J., *The Destruction of the Dutch Jews* (E.P. Dutton 1969), p. 70.
4. Schrabauer, Andreas, *"...und der Block war judenleer" Die NS-Verfolgung von Juden in den Niederlanden und ihre Ermordung in Konzentrationslager Mauthausen* (new academic press, Wien Hamburg 2021), pp. 77–79. The book is Volume 15 of Mauthausen Studies, a Series of Papers by the Mauthausen Memorial Council. Ms. Katharina Kniefacz is listed as an editor and proofreader for the series of papers. The information about Andreas appears to be lifted verbatim from a very early draft of the family history that Mom submitted to the Leo Baeck Institute, unbeknownst to me.

3. Mauthausen Concentration Camp

1. *Mauthausen 8.8.1938–5.5.1945* (Östereichische Lagergemeinschaft Mauthausen 1996), hereafter Official Guide.
2. Eckstein, Benjamin, *Jews in the Mauthausen Concentration Camp*, published as part of *The Nazi Concentration Camps, Structure and Aims, The Image of the Prisoner, The Jews in the Camps, Fifth Session* (Yad Vashem 1980), p. 257.
3. Ibid., p. 258.
4. www.mauthausen-memorial.org/en/History/
5. Ibid. Official Guide pp. 7-8.
6. Eckstein, p. 264; see also Le Chêne, Evelyn, *Mauthausen, The History of a Death Camp* (Methuen 1971), pp. 110–112 (describing brutal treatment of Dutch prisoners and citing eyewitness accounts).
7. Official Guide, p. 15.
8. Kogon, Eugen, *Der SS-Staat. Das System der Deutschen Konzentrationlager* (1946, Berlin), translation from German, *The Theory and Practice of Hell* (Berkley Book), 1950, p. 180.
9. Bernadac, Christian, *The 186 Steps, Mauthausen* (Ferni Publ. House 1978), p. 186.

10. Horowitz, Gordon J., *In the Shadow of Death: Living Outside the Gates of Mauthausen* (N.Y. FreePress 1990), p. 17; Official Guide, p. 11 (description of "Execution Corner").

11. Horowitz, pp. 60–62.

12. www.mauthausen-memorial.org/en/History/

13. Horowitz, pp. 41, 53-54.

14. Ibid., p. 35

15. www.mauthausen-memorial.org/en/History/

16. Le Chêne, p. 116.

17. Official Guide, p. 8. The Mauthausen Memorial website states around 190,000 people were imprisoned and "at least" 90,000 were killed at Mauthausen. The USHMM estimates 197,464 prisoners, with "at least" 95,000 who died in the Mauthausen camp system.
    www.ushmm.org/wlc/en/article.php?ModuleId=10005196.

4. Pilgrimage to Mauthausen, 1998

1. For photos of Mauthausen camp, quarry and death steps during the Nazi era: Jankowski, Matthew L., *Atrocities at Camp Mauthausen: A Visual Documentation of the Holocaust* (Shiffer Publ. 2003); www.holocaustresearchproject.org/other-camps/galleries/mautgal2/index.html; www.jewishgen.org/Forgotten-Camps/Camps/MauthausenEng.html; www.holocaustresearchproject.org/other-camps/mauthausen.html; Mom's binders on Mauthausen also include many photos of the camp from 1938 through 1945.

2. Official Guide, pp. 10, 13 ("During the night of February 16, 1945, at least 200 prisoners, among them General Karbyshev, were forced to stand outside while cold water was being poured over them. None of them survived the torture." Some 4,300 prisoners, mostly Soviet officers who had escaped from POW camps and been recaptured, were sent to Mauthausen for execution. However, most of these prisoners were left to starve to death.)

5. Georg Fröhlich and Edith Nissen

1. Schröeder, Peter, *Georg Fröhlich, President of the Regional Court in Münster*, published in Westfälische Jurisprudenz (1999) (article written for the 50th anniversary of the Westfalian Jurisprudence Association that our grandfather re-instituted in 1949 while a judge in Münster). Schröeder wrote that Georg was assigned as an inspector because health issues precluded him from the battlefront, but did not specify the health reasons. Information about Georg's legal career also comes from a two-page autobiography Georg wrote dated May 16, 1951.

6. Childhood of Andreas and Sabine

1. This childhood perception of a "poor people's smell" sounded snobbish and cringeworthy, unlike our egalitarian mother. I thought a more plausible explanation was that the smell was that of a dampish basement dwelling but when we visited Sabine's childhood home in 2016, we saw it was not a basement dwelling, but rather a ground floor apartment that now serves as the office of an architecture firm. So my assumption of basement mold smell was wrong. Sabine did have an enhanced sense of smell, like a bloodhound. No matter where my brothers hid to smoke, she could sniff them out.

2. Bruno Sonnabend became a judge in the German federal court of justice after the war. The other junior lawyer the Fröhlichs reconnected with after the war was Bernhard Wieczorek.

7. Germany, 1930–38

1. www.google.com/books/edition/Jews_and_Other_Germans/3Rrl8qAhzlMC? hl=en&gbpv=1&bsq=freemason (Jews were members of the Breslau Freemasons).

2. Wernicke, Konrad, *Jugendjahre im Schatten des NS-Regimes, Erinnerungen eines Schlesischen Juristen* (Würtzburg Bergstadtverlag, Korn 1995), pp. 106–107, 130.

3. Ascher, Abraham, *A Community Under Siege. The Jews of Breslau under Nazism* (Stanford University Press, 2007). My brother Chris arranged a phone call between Sabine and Ascher sometime after the book was published in 2007 and they shared memories about Breslau.

4. Ibid., pp. 20–21.

5. Ibid. pp. 21, 60

6. Ibid, pp. 76–78.

7. Ibid., p. 80.

8. Fröhlich, Georg, *"Abschrift Lebenlauf,"* 16.5.1951 (Münster).

9. Ascher, p. 112.

10. "The decree named items to be declared: Property, cash, securities, insurance policies, pension plans, mortgages, material assets such as coal, electric power, or supplies of rye (for bread), jewelry and all other luxuries. The completed forms were due on June 30, although the authorities granted extensions and some came in as late as February 1939... In all, 4,891 declarations had been submitted, 4,324 in Breslau itself and 567 in neighboring districts. The assets were divided into four categories: land and forests, landed property, businesses, and other items of value." Ibid., pp. 128, 131.

8. Sabine's Memories of the Rise of Nazism

1. Sudetenland used to be part of Germany, but was partitioned to Czechoslovakia after WWI. Great Britain, France and Italy appeased Hitler's demands as part of the Munich Agreement, allowing German annexation of Sudetenland. The Czechoslovak government was not consulted, and lacking support from other nations, submitted to the annexation.

2. Nissen, Rudolf, *Helle Blätter-Dunkle Blätter, Erinnerungen eines Chirurgen* (Deutsche Verlags-Anstalt 1969), pp. 191–192. For articles about Dr. Nissen's distinguished surgical career: clinicalanatomy.com/100-mtd/338-rudolf-nissen-md; Fults, D.W., Taussky, P., *The Life of Rudolf Nissen: Advancing surgery through science and principle,* ncbi.nlm.nih.gov/pubmed/21424871; Batirel, H., Yüksel, M., *Rudolf Nissen's Years in Bosphorus and the Pioneers of Thoracic Surgery in Turkey,* annalsthoracicsurgery.org/article/S0003-4975(99)01480-0/pdf; whonamedit.com/doctor.cfm/2594.html

3. Heidenberger, Peter, *From Munich to Washington D.C.* (Xlibris 2004), p. 105. After the war, Georg became Peter's sponsor for his doctoral thesis about the Dachau War Crimes trials.

4. Information about Ferdi Nissen's family is from Beate's unpublished "A Brief History of My Early Years" (1999) and my interview with her in 2015. Information about Rudi's family is from his autobiography, supra.

9. Kristallnacht, The Night of Broken Glass

1. Ascher., pp. 170, 171.
2. Ibid., p. 183.

10. Nazi Edicts after Kristallnacht: The Vise tightens

1. Ibid., pp. 173, 175, 176.
2. Ibid., p. 121.
3. Ibid., pp. 187, 197, 199.
4. Ibid., p. 203.

11. Sabine and Andreas evacuated to England

1. Later, Herman Heineman was rearrested and released again. He would not leave Germany until his brother Otto was released. The Heineman family then left, crossing the border to Vaals. They spent a few days in Vaals at the monastery with Pater Adams before leaving for England to await visas to the United States. Other members of the Heineman family left for Cuba and South America. A brother-in-law, Fritz, went to Ecuador, and through his connections would later help the Fröhlichs obtain visas to travel there.

2. Sabine gave me the little pink suitcase, but I didn't appreciate its significance at the time. It molded and disintegrated in my basement. I feel very guilty about that and wish I had thought to preserve and donate it to a Holocaust museum.

3. According to Sabine, the Kinnaird Park School no longer exists and even the name of the street it was on has been changed.

4. In boxes of Fröhlich photographs, I found small pictures of the campus of St. Edmund's, with notations in neat script on the back stating that they were taken in June 1939. I do not recognize the handwriting on the photos or know who took them and sent them to the Fröhlichs. The St. Edmund's pictures include a small photo of an unidentified couple, possibly the Smiths.

13. WWII starts, trapping the Fröhlichs

1. A nephew of Georg Fröhlich was interned as an enemy alien in England, then sent to Australia where he died of pneumonia. Ludwig Meisner, a painter and boarding school classmate of Georg, was also interned in England during the war.

15. The Germans invade, Andreas murdered in Mauthausen

1. The map is on display at The Dutch Resistance Museum in Amsterdam. When I visited the museum in 2014, I saw the map had a black dot on Prins Hendriklaan and it took my breath away, as I realized the Fröhlichs and other Jewish residents would have been unaware they had already been marked as targets for the Nazis. Each dot a bullseye for annihilation.

2. Herzberg, *Kroniek der Joden-vervolging*, pp. 69–71.

17. Sabine in Hiding, Edith's Arrest

1. Though Edith faked a heart attack, the stress of the arrest did have health consequences. Postwar, a Prof. Dr. E.S Lacquer signed a declaration, dated March 11, 1946, that after Mrs. Fröhlich was arrested by the green police, she became very seriously ill and placed herself under his care. Through that care, the doctor wrote, he became acquainted with her great and very understandable hatred of the Nazi regime.

18. Return to Amsterdam, the "Worst Time"

1. The Arolsen archives confirm that a Victor Manheimer from Berlin, born Dec. 7, 1877, lived at Prins Hendriklaan 36 in Amsterdam-Zuid and died on Dec. 10, 1942. The Joods Monument records that Manheimer was a philosophy professor who committed suicide by jumping from the Joodsche Schouwburg. The Dutch

Resistance managed to smuggle lots of children out from this site and into hiding. The theater is now a museum, but only part of the original wall is left.

21. A Series of Hiding Places and Meeting Cor Schipper

1. The ulcers Sabine described having at the Crijnsen farm would be consistent with cutaneous diphtheria. cdc.gov/diphtheria/clinicians.html and cdc.gov/diphtheria/about/symptoms.html
2. westfriesgenootschap.nl/geschiedschrijving/biografie/biografie_samuel_wytema.php

22. The Schipper and Buis Families

1. On the Schipper side, from a list in Dad's handwriting: Tenis H. Schipper (S) (b. Dec. 12, 1699); Jacob S. (b. May 29, 1733); Jan S. (b. Dec. 12, 1759); Cornelis S. (b. July 25, 1791); Cornelis S. (b. Sept. 23, 1834); Cornelis S. (b. May 23, 1859); Klaas S. (b. April 4, 1888). On the Buis side: Pieter Buis (b. 1795); Johannes Buis (b. 1834); Jacob Buis (1867–1938); Maria Elizabeth Buis (1890–1975).

23. Oom Cor arrested, Hidden Persons relocated

1. Chris had been contacted in 2017 by Sander M.A. Baker a Dutch writer of local history, who was researching a story about Dad's uncle Cor as a forgotten war hero. Sander passed on a number of questions for Chris to ask Dad, including whether Dad had seen Oom Cor after the arrest. Dad, perhaps typical for his generation, always seemed to have an easier time conversing with his sons than with his daughters. My questions about his war experiences were frequently deflected. Chris was able to elicit more details from Dad about those war years than I ever could. In 2018, Sander succeeded in his mission to have the Westwoud township name a pathway after the senior Cor Schipper. The article is available to read at www.facebook.com/HetGeheugenVanWestwoud/posts/2012426755659063:0]
2. *In Bovenkarspel staat een huis... Een dagboek over Huize Elastiek, 1944–1945* (In Bovenkarspel stands a house... A diary about House Elastic 1944–1945) by Georg Fröhlich and Willy Elders (McNally Jackson Books, New York 2017), www.houseelastic.com.

26. Cor's Work with the Mandrill Resistance Cell

1. An article about the Mandrill unit, including a map of the Mandrill field and pictures of the Mandrill farmhouse is available here:

www.westfriesgenootschap.nl/archivering/west-
friesland_toen_en_nu/wf_ten_07_58_59.php
2. *Aflevering: Wapendroppings in Noord Holland,* Andere Tijden (anderetijden.nl).
   www.anderetijden.nl/programma/1/Andere-Tijden/aflever-
   ing/10/Wapendroppings-in-Noord-Holland

ACKNOWLEDGMENTS

I owe thanks to several people who made the publication of this family history possible:

My brother Chris who provided his own research, source material and photos.

Bill Weinberger who helped translate documents from German to English.

Jill Weinberger who read early drafts and provided helpful suggestions.

John Carson for his support and encouragement.

My sister Doortje for photos and brother André for scanning photos.

My cousin Klaas Buijsman who arranged a tour in North Holland of places where my mother and her parents were hidden and where my father worked in the Mandrill Resistance cell.

Stephen Falk for sharing his genealogy research, Alice Harris for her genealogy work into my mother's ancestors and my cousin Peter Greene for creating a digital family tree.

Tom Feltham for his editing.

And especially Liesbeth Heenk of Amsterdam Publishers for accepting my manuscript and being willing to take a chance on publishing it.

My apologies to anyone who feels they should be on this list but isn't. Let me know who you are in case there is a second edition.

FURTHER READING AMSTERDAM PUBLISHERS

The series **Holocaust Survivor Memoirs World War II** by Amsterdam Publishers consists of the following autobiographies of survivors:

Outcry. Holocaust Memoirs, by Manny Steinberg

Hank Brodt Holocaust Memoirs. A Candle and a Promise, by Deborah Donnelly

The Dead Years. Holocaust Memoirs, by Joseph Schupack

Rescued from the Ashes. The Diary of Leokadia Schmidt, Survivor of the Warsaw Ghetto, by Leokadia Schmidt

My Lvov. Holocaust Memoir of a twelve-year-old Girl, by Janina Hescheles

Remembering Ravensbrück. From Holocaust to Healing, by Natalie Hess

Wolf. A Story of Hate, by Zeev Scheinwald with Ella Scheinwald

Save my Children. An Astonishing Tale of Survival and its Unlikely Hero, by Leon Kleiner with Edwin Stepp

Holocaust Memoirs of a Bergen-Belsen Survivor & Classmate of Anne Frank, by Nanette Blitz Konig

Defiant German - Defiant Jew. A Holocaust Memoir from inside the Third Reich, by Walter Leopold with Les Leopold

In a Land of Forest and Darkness. The Holocaust Story of two Jewish Partisans, by Sara Lustigman Omelinski

Holocaust Memories. Annihilation and Survival in Slovakia, by Paul Davidovits

From Auschwitz with Love. The Inspiring Memoir of Two Sisters' Survival, Devotion and Triumph Told by Manci Grunberger Beran & Ruth Grunberger Mermelstein, by Daniel Seymour

Remetz. Resistance Fighter and Survivor of the Warsaw Ghetto, by Jan Yohay Remetz

---

The series **Holocaust Survivor True Stories WWII** by Amsterdam Publishers consists of the following biographies:

Among the Reeds. The true story of how a family survived the Holocaust, by Tammy Bottner

A Holocaust Memoir of Love & Resilience. Mama's Survival from Lithuania to America, by Ettie Zilber

Living among the Dead. My Grandmother's Holocaust Survival Story of Love and Strength, by Adena Bernstein Astrowsky

Heart Songs. A Holocaust Memoir, by Barbara Gilford

Shoes of the Shoah. The Tomorrow of Yesterday, by Dorothy Pierce

Hidden in Berlin. A Holocaust Memoir, by Evelyn Joseph Grossman

Separated Together. The Incredible True WWII Story of Soulmates Stranded an Ocean Apart, by Kenneth P. Price, Ph.D.

The Man Across the River. The incredible story of one man's will to survive the Holocaust, by Zvi Wiesenfeld

If Anyone Calls, Tell Them I Died. A Memoir, by Emanuel (Manu) Rosen

The House on Thrömerstrasse. A Story of Rebirth and Renewal in the Wake of the Holocaust, by Ron Vincent

Dancing with my Father. His hidden past. Her quest for truth. How Nazi Vienna shaped a family's identity, by Jo Sorochinsky

The Story Keeper. Weaving the Threads of Time and Memory - A Memoir, by Fred Feldman

Krisia's Silence. The Girl who was not on Schindler's List, by Ronny Hein

Defying Death on the Danube. A Holocaust Survival Story, by Debbie J. Callahan with Henry Stern

A Doorway to Heroism. A decorated German-Jewish Soldier who became an American Hero, by Rabbi W. Jack Romberg

The Shoemaker's Son. The Life of a Holocaust Resister, by Laura Beth Bakst

The Redhead of Auschwitz. A True Story, by Nechama Birnbaum

Land of Many Bridges. My Father's Story, by Bela Ruth Samuel Tenenholtz

Creating Beauty from the Abyss. The Amazing Story of Sam Herciger, Auschwitz Survivor and Artist, by Lesley Ann Richardson

On Sunny Days We Sang. A Holocaust Story of Survival and Resilience, by Jeannette Grunhaus de Gelman

Painful Joy. A Holocaust Family Memoir, by Max J. Friedman

I Give You My Heart. A True Story of Courage and Survival, by Wendy Holden

Flower of Vlora. Growing up Jewish in Communist Albania, by Anna Kohen

Zaidy's War, by Martin Bodek

In the Time of Madmen, by Mark A. Prelas

The series **Jewish Children in the Holocaust** by Amsterdam Publishers consists of the following autobiographies of Jewish children hidden during WWII in the Netherlands:

Searching for Home. The Impact of WWII on a Hidden Child, by Joseph Gosler

See You Tonight and Promise to be a Good Boy! War memories, by Salo Muller

Sounds from Silence. Reflections of a Child Holocaust Survivor, Psychiatrist and Teacher, by Robert Krell

Sabine's Odyssey. A Hidden Child and her Dutch Rescuers, by Agnes Schipper

The Journey of a Hidden Child, by Harry Pila with Robin Black

---

The series **New Jewish Fiction** by Amsterdam Publishers consists of the following novels, written by Jewish authors. All novels are set in the time during or after the Holocaust.

The Corset Maker. A Novel, by Annette Libeskind Berkovits

Escaping the Whale. The Holocaust is over. But is it ever over for the next generation? by Ruth Rotkowitz

When the Music Stopped. Willy Rosen's Holocaust, by Casey Hayes

Hands of Gold. One Man's Quest to Find the Silver Lining in Misfortune, by Roni Robbins

There was a garden in Nuremberg. A Novel, by Navina Michal Clemerson

Aftermath: Coming-of-Age on Three Continents, by Annette Libeskind Berkovits

The Girl Who Counted Numbers, by Roslyn Bernstein

The Butterfly and the Axe, by Omer Bartov

The series **Holocaust Books for Young Adults** by Amsterdam Publishers consists of the following novels, based on true stories:

A Life in Shelter, by Suzette Sheft

The Boy behind the Door. How Salomon Kool Escaped the Nazis, by David Tabatsky

The Precious Few. An Inspirational Saga of Courage based on True Stories, by David Twain with Art Twain

ABOUT THE AUTHOR

Agnes Schipper. Photo by Suzanne Perreault of Blakely of Suzanne Blakely Photography

Agnes Schipper is the daughter of a hidden child and a member of the Dutch Resistance who helped save her mother from the Holocaust. Born in New York City, Agnes was raised as a Catholic, the faith of her parents, and first learned about her mother's hidden Jewish ancestry when she was 20. Agnes had a career as a newspaper reporter and editor and later as an attorney. Retirement allowed her the time to research and write about her parents' remarkable story. The mother of four and grandmother of five, Agnes lives in Sarasota, Florida.

CPSIA information can be obtained
at www.ICGtesting.com
Printed in the USA
LVHW101909290422
717236LV00073B/1419/J

9 789493 231955